A RESTFUL MIND

HAZELDEN MEDITATIONS

A RESTFUL MIND

DAILY MEDITATIONS
FOR ENHANCING MENTAL HEALTH

Mark Allen Zabawa

HAZELDEN®

Hazelden
Center City, Minnesota 55012
hazelden.org

Library of Congress Cataloging-in-Publication Data

Zabawa, Mark Allen, 1960–
A restful mind : daily meditations for enhancing mental
health / Mark Allen Zabawa.
   p.   cm. — (Hazelden meditations)
Includes index.
ISBN 978-1-59285-752-4 (softcover)
1. Meditation—Therapeutic use. 2. Mental health. I. Title
RC489.M42Z33 2010
615.8'52—dc22

                                        2009049788

14 13 12 11 10 1 2 3 4 5 6

Cover design by David Spohn
Interior design by David Spohn
Typesetting by BookMobile Design and Publishing Services,
   Minneapolis, Minnesota.

On your journey ahead you will find yourself discovering limitations that you will grow to accept and possibilities far reaching your imagination. You will learn to accept and cope with your illness and realize that it does not define you as an individual, but rather it is one part of your true being.

—MARK ALLEN ZABAWA

• F O R E W O R D •

Recovery from mental illness is a process. It means taking care of ourselves each and every day—spiritually, emotionally, and physically. It means actively working to make change. It means making health and stability a priority. Although we each recover in our own way and on our own schedule, we all need help, and help comes in many forms.

Some of us go to therapy, for example. Many of us use prescription medication under the care of a doctor. Some of us attend regular support group meetings and work with mentors or sponsors. These and the many other ways we take care of ourselves are sometimes called the *tools of recovery*. We choose the ones that work best for us.

Millions of people in recovery from various illnesses have used a tool called bibliotherapy, which means reading to promote growth and understanding. A meditation book, like this one, is a common form of bibliotherapy. Because it can help with immediate issues, it works like an aspirin. Because it promotes psychological and spiritual growth, it works like a vitamin. Like other recovery tools, it works best when used on a regular basis.

A Restful Mind is a testament to experience, strength, and hope. Its daily meditations speak to all of us, regardless of our diagnosis. Topics include having setbacks, reducing anxiety, taking medication, asking for help, experiencing inpatient treatment, and being gentle with ourselves. Each one-page meditation has three parts: a reflection, a question to promote awareness, and a thought for the day. It helps to read each meditation more than once.

We read a meditation book like this one for many reasons. It can offer reassurance. It can help us feel normal. It can help us see where we've been and where we want to go. It can help us think more clearly and understand ourselves better. Though not every topic may seem to apply to our situation on any given day, we can still gain new insights and perspectives on mental illness from the ideas and experiences of others.

Like doing anything new, reading this book might feel strange at first. Be sure to give it a fair chance. Use it to start your day or end your day. Or carry it with you and read it when you have time. The idea is to make reading this book a daily ritual on your recovery journey. The goal is growth, support, and understanding.

Reading a meditation is like listening to someone who knows us and accepts us even though we have never met. With time, may *A Restful Mind* become a comfort, a companion, and a touchstone for you.

—Tim Mc, author of *Today I Will Do One Thing*

A RESTFUL MIND

JANUARY

• J A N U A R Y   1 •

A New Year, a New Beginning

As the new year begins, we may be tempted to look back and focus on what we fell short of accomplishing, rather than looking at all that we have accomplished. We may sense failure for not completing every task we began. Or we may feel let down because some of what we wanted to have happen did not.

Let us be gentle with ourselves, however, for this is a new year and a new beginning. Let us look to our past for wisdom and guidance rather than failure and someone to blame. Let us look at what we achieved rather than at what failed to happen.

As we begin the new year, let us move forward with faith, courage, and the willingness to learn from each of our experiences. Let us focus on opportunities. But most of all, let us be true to ourselves and our recovery.

Am I stuck on last year or can I begin the new year today with faith and an open mind?

Thought for the Day

Today is a new beginning.

✹

MENTAL ILLNESS IS NOT A WEAKNESS

Mental illness is not a moral or psychological weakness. We are not weak-willed, defective, or underdeveloped. Mental illness is a biochemical illness that can affect anyone at any time.

As we continue our journey, it is important to remember that our illness has nothing to do with our character, personality, economic status, willingness, nor any other mythological cause.

Today, am I clear about who I am and the source of my illness?

THOUGHT FOR THE DAY

I have an illness, not a weakness of the mind or soul.

SUCCESS

We often think that success is based on how much money we have or what we possess or our status in the community. But for those of us with a mental illness, success is more often defined by our ability to cope with our illness.

Many of us have turned what seemed an impossible situation into a new way of living. Some of us have returned to work. Most of us have gained a better understanding of ourselves. Many of us have achieved some goals and dreams.

On our journey we will have many opportunities for success. If today we have begun to manage our illness and take back our life, we have already tasted it.

Today, do I realize that success is already a part of my life?

THOUGHT FOR THE DAY

*I can succeed day after day by learning
to cope with and manage my illness.*

✳

OUR LIVES CAN CHANGE

Our lives can change if we let them. Once we have been lifted from the depths of despair and are no longer prisoners of our illness, we will have opportunities to achieve things we once thought impossible. We will find the courage and strength to cope with each day. Hopelessness will be replaced with hope and faith. We will learn that we are not alone and that others are willing to help us. We will come to know ourselves and accept ourselves as we are—not merely for what we think we should become. We will know serenity and become at peace with the world around us.

Do I believe my life can change today? Am I willing to let positive changes happen?

THOUGHT FOR THE DAY

*Sometimes positive change is an act of will,
and sometimes it's just letting good things happen.*

✳

FOCUSING ON SOLUTIONS

If we are to learn to cope with our illness and our life, we must begin focusing on solutions, not just on our problems.

But this means we must change our attitude and outlook. We can no longer live as if there are only problems in our lives. We can no longer consider ourselves victims and hold on to the attitude that our life will never change. Nor can we continue to be consumed by self-pity. If so, we will fail to take responsibility for finding solutions. We will continue to live within what we have grown to know so well: our problems.

Do I let my problems define me today or do I seek solutions?

THOUGHT FOR THE DAY

For every problem there is a solution.

AN HONEST LIFE

If we have not yet admitted to ourselves and to others that we have a mental illness, we must do so now. We cannot live a lie. We must stand tall and be honest about who we are, including both our strengths and our limitations.

Let us put fear, embarrassment, and shame aside and let faith, trust, and courage guide us to a life of truth.

Do I live today in the truth of who I am?

THOUGHT FOR THE DAY

If I admit who I am, I invite healing and acceptance.

HAVING A VISION

As we progress on our journey, it is critical that we have goals and dreams and continually seek direction for our recovery and our life. We need a vision that begins within us and expands into the world; a vision that gives us energy to wake up each day and move forward.

Whether our vision is one of health, spirituality, belonging, or improving the world—or anything else worthwhile—it belongs to us. It may become our life's work and perhaps the essence of who we are. Our vision can help us heal and become a force for good in the world.

Do I have a vision for my life today?

THOUGHT FOR THE DAY

A vision feeds the soul.

AVOIDING SELF-CENTEREDNESS

With a mental illness, we sometimes need to be selfish for the sake of our recovery. Yet recovery need not take up all twenty-four hours in a day. When we're feeling strong, we can share our strength with people who need it. When we're feeling fragile, we don't try to be heroes and risk compromising our own health.

Instead, we strive for balance between caring for ourselves and caring for others.

Do I live only for others today or do I strive for balance?

THOUGHT FOR THE DAY

In caring for myself I am caring for others.

• J A N U A R Y   9 •

UNDERSTANDING OUR ILLNESS

Many of us have experienced our illness for some time. It is always with us. It may fade but it always returns. It tests our patience often. It takes away dreams. Even as we fight it with all our strength, we try to accept it each day.

Sometimes our illness has complete control over us. Sometimes it is more gentle. We feel moments of madness and periods of sanity.

Over time, we have come to accept that although our illness is part of us, it is not *all* of us. Our life continues well beyond the limits of our illness. *And* we will go on living as best we can, with hope, faith, and the guidance of our Higher Power.

Have I begun to understand and accept my illness today?

THOUGHT FOR THE DAY

Understanding my illness helps me managed it and cope with it.

WHEN SELFISHNESS IS A MUST

One form of selfishness is a positive force in our lives. It is directed toward our health and recovery. It is about putting our emotional, physical, and spiritual health first. It is about managing and coping with our illness.

Being selfish in this way means taking responsibility for ourselves and taking care of ourselves. It means knowing when to say yes and when to say no. It means doing what we need to do for our health, rather than doing whatever we want and risking our health and possibly our lives.

When it comes to managing my illness and recovery, am I appropriately selfish today?

THOUGHT FOR THE DAY

A selfishness that puts my health
and recovery first is a must.

OLD TAPES OR NEW TAPES?

The old mental tapes many of us play can be destructive and self-defeating. Some tapes we made ourselves; with others, we had help.

Regardless of who made our mental tapes, they will hold us back in recovery if we do not replace them. Just as we created these negative tapes, we can make new ones that contain messages of love and caring, messages that tell us we deserve good things in our lives, messages that we can cope with and use to manage our illness.

The choice is ours. We can keep playing our old self-destructive tapes or we can begin to make and play new, positive, healthy ones.

Which tapes do I play today?

THOUGHT FOR THE DAY

I cannot magically make my illness go away, but I can support my recovery through healthy self-talk.

• J A N U A R Y 1 2 •

NEW IDEAS

Accepting new ideas can be difficult when it comes to managing our illness. But if we reject them, we deny ourselves a chance to feel better physically, emotionally, and spiritually.

We need to be open to new ideas, new ways of doing things, new forms of treatment. There are no guarantees, but if what we are doing now isn't working well, it makes sense to try something different.

Let us be open to new ideas—not only about our illness, but about life itself.

Am I open to trying new ideas and approaches today?

THOUGHT FOR THE DAY

Though there is some risk in trying new ideas,
the possibilities for gain far outweigh it.

Hospitalized or Committed

Many of us with mental illness have been hospitalized or committed for our illness, perhaps more than once. Perhaps we felt ashamed or embarrassed.

Yet no matter how unpleasant, it probably saved us from harm—and may have saved our lives. Certainly it saved us from our illness and from destructive behavior.

There is no need for embarrassment or shame about an act that saved our health or our life. Hospitalization or legal commitment protects us; it is not a punishment nor a sentence. It allows us to get healthier. It is a step toward recovery.

Today, do I see the value of hospitalization or commitment should I need it?

Thought for the Day

*I do whatever it takes to get better,
including hospitalization if it is needed.*

Easy to Run, Hard to Stay

At times our fear and pain may seem unbearable. Our instinct may be to run, to retreat and avoid the fear and pain.

Yet if we can learn to stay and cope with the situation and our feelings, if we have the desire and the willingness, things can improve. Running may become our second option. As we begin to face and cope with our life, we will discover that it is actually much easier to stay than run.

Do I run from situations and feelings today, or do I stay and cope with them?

Thought for the Day

Whenever I run, all that I am running from will eventually catch up to me, and I will find myself right back where I was.

SLIPPING

As we begin healing emotionally, physically, and spiritually, and begin managing our illness with some success, we may start to think we will never have another slip. But such thinking is dangerous. The only way to cope with our illness is one day at a time.

Chances are, there will be times of difficulty or crisis. We must prepare ourselves in the event that our illness takes hold of us. It is like practicing to escape a fire, while hoping and praying that a fire never occurs.

We need to remember that having a slip is not the end of the world. When we slip, we pull ourselves together and move forward again. But if we tell ourselves we'll never fall again, then it will be that much harder when we do.

Do I believe that I will never slip backward again or do I face the realities of my illness today?

THOUGHT FOR THE DAY

Rather than fear the inevitable, I prepare for it.

FOCUSING

Many of us have had a difficult time focusing on anything but our illness and its symptoms. Perhaps we concluded that we were losing our minds.

But we need not panic. Yes, we are affected by the symptoms of our illness. However, as we learn to manage our illness and cope with its symptoms, we will be able to focus on the tasks at hand once again.

For many of us, this process will take time and patience. But it can be done, one day at a time.

Can I focus my thoughts on the tasks at hand today?

THOUGHT FOR THE DAY

I need not panic, but have faith that, day by day, I will be able to focus my thoughts once again.

• J A N U A R Y   1 7 •

LIVING ONE DAY AT A TIME

Upon awakening each day, we ask our Higher Power to guide us in making healthy choices and coping with our illness as best as we can. We ask to know the will of this Power and that we may be guided to others who may need our help. We ask for courage and wisdom to face each situation that is put before us. We ask for courage and wisdom to do the right thing.

After we have sought guidance from our Higher Power, we are ready to walk forward in faith and courage, knowing that we will not be alone for the twenty-four hours that lie ahead.

Do I seek guidance from my Higher Power today?

THOUGHT FOR THE DAY

*Today's twenty-four hours are mine
to live and to cherish.*

FEAR AND FAITH

For many of us, fear is one of our strongest barriers to recovery. We fear our illness, ourselves, our futures, and more. Fear can paralyze us, keep us isolated, keep us from accepting our illness, and keep us from reaching our dreams.

The opposite of fear is faith. When we build faith, fear loses the power it once had. The only way to build faith is one situation at a time. Each time we face fear, act in spite of it, and things work out, we build more faith—both in ourselves and in our Higher Power.

We will all continue to encounter situations that we fear. But with faith, we can cope with our fears one by one.

Can I use faith to cope with my fears today?

THOUGHT FOR THE DAY

When I face my fears, I grow stronger.

COMING OUT OF ISOLATION

For those of us with a mental illness, isolation has been a friend. We have come to know what it is like to go for hours, days, and weeks living entirely within ourselves. We know what it is like to shut everything and everyone out of our lives. It is comforting, but it can also be dangerous. It can alienate us from the people who care about us.

But isolation is no longer necessary. There is a happy and sane middle ground. We can find a place of solitude and comfort where we can be by ourselves and remain sane, yet know and appreciate the company of others. It is a place where we can have friends and can be called a friend.

Can I come out of isolation today and connect with others?

THOUGHT FOR THE DAY

When I come out of isolation,
I gain freedom and friendship.

LONELINESS CAN BE LIFTED

Many of us have been to the bottom of the blackest hole of loneliness—some for weeks, some for months or years. But no matter how far down we go, we are not doomed to loneliness.

There is no magic wand that can make our loneliness suddenly disappear. It goes away when we accept the fact that we are lonely and begin taking responsibility for it. We need to reach out to others when we want and need their company. We are the only ones who can end our loneliness.

If I am lonely today, do I stay alone and stuck or do I seek out other people?

THOUGHT FOR THE DAY

I am certain to have times of loneliness on my journey, but it need not be permanent if I reach out.

SLOWLY CHANGING HOW WE THINK AND ACT

No matter our illness or addiction, our first step in recovery is to get it under control as best we can. Our second step is to change how we think and act.

We must change ourselves to meet the new conditions that our life dictates. We must work toward balance. Before we act, we must always think of the consequences. We may also need to make changes in how we approach work, play, friends, or family.

These changes will not happen overnight. They involve a process that takes effort, patience, and prayer. They may even take us a step or two backward. But over time, we can change how we think and act to support and manage the new reality of our life.

Am I willing to begin thinking and acting differently today?

THOUGHT FOR THE DAY

Changing behavior is like learning to ride a bicycle.
I may skin my knees a few times at first,
but eventually I learn to ride.

CRYING OUT FOR HELP

Chances are, most of us have done a lot of crying inside and praying for help. But often we found no relief or answers. The hours and days we spent on our knees seemed in vain.

What we failed to recognize is that we were only crying inside. No one came to help because we didn't cry out to those who could hear our pain and answer.

Today, we must connect with those who can hear us and who are willing to help.

If I am in pain and need help today, can I reach out to others?

THOUGHT FOR THE DAY

Learning to ask for help is a skill
that needs to be developed.

THE ROAD LESS TRAVELED

We have chosen a life of recovery from our illness rather than giving in to it. It is not an easy road; it is the road less traveled. We have already begun to see that it is the only road worth taking. No other way of living with our illness will suffice.

Today, do I search for an easier, softer way or do I continue to choose the hard work of recovery?

THOUGHT FOR THE DAY

*For my life with mental illness,
there is no better road than the road of recovery.*

FEAR OF SYMPTOMS

Facing the symptoms of our illness can be frightening. There will be times on our journey when the road we have chosen looks dark and difficult, and what lies ahead looks unbearable. Self-doubt may turn into hopelessness. We may wish we had chosen an easier road.

Yet we go forth in spite of our fear. And from these times and from these dark roads we gain strength and wisdom. Many others have done so before us. So can we.

If my symptoms are bad today, how do I respond?

THOUGHT FOR THE DAY

*The darkest roads will sometimes be
part of my journey. But when I go forth
with faith and courage, I can find my way.*

• J A N U A R Y   2 5 •

Giving Away Our Gift

By working a recovery plan, we have found a gift.
We have learned to manage our illness and its symptoms with some success. In the process, we have
begun to gain wisdom, courage, peace of mind, and
a new way of life.

Many of us remember a time when we were desperate for these things, but they were nowhere to be
found. Then we met other people like us.

When two people with similar illnesses share
with each other, we don't have to make excuses or
explain everything. We have a common bond and a
common goal: coping with our illnesses and living
our lives to the fullest. Giving what we have found
to others helps us keep what we desperately wanted
and now have.

Today, do I graciously share what I have learned?

Thought for the Day

*My recovery depends on giving away
what I have learned.*

Doing the Right Thing

It is difficult to do the right thing, to make the honorable decision in every circumstance. None of us have been granted perfection.

But this should not hinder our striving to do the right thing every day of our journey. If we think about doing the right thing consistently, this thinking will become a part of us over time. We will always be thinking of our morals, our values, and of course, a spiritual way of life. We will not make the healthiest decisions all the time, but more often than not, they will be good ones.

Today, do I act compulsively or do I stop and think about doing the right thing?

Thought for the Day

Over time, doing the right thing will make me the person I want to be.

BOTH FEET IN REALITY

There are days when it is difficult to keep both feet in reality, in the here and now. It seems easier to have one foot in yesterday and one in tomorrow. But that leaves today unknown.

If we are to live in reality, we must learn to touch and feel what is in our lives this very moment. We must begin looking for wisdom and strength and avoid looking back at what should have been or looking ahead to what we want to have happen.

When we keep both feet in today, we will find far more life than in our perceptions of yesterday and tomorrow combined.

Today, do I live in the here and now?

THOUGHT FOR THE DAY

Let me live in what is real.
Let me live in the here and now.
Let me keep both feet in today.

FINDING OUR WAY

Today is a journey toward managing our illness, a journey toward acceptance of a Higher Power and of ourselves, a journey toward a better tomorrow.

Sometimes we will stumble and fall; at other times we will face little resistance. We will find opportunities for growth, acceptance, and change. If we remain patient and seek direction from our Higher Power, we will find our way.

Today, do I realize that life is a journey, and that each step helps me find my way to the next?

THOUGHT FOR THE DAY

My journey is unique and sometimes unpredictable.
Yet I will not lose my way if I stay open
and pay attention.

BELONGING

For a period of time we may have lost our purpose in life. We could see only that our life had been taken away by our illness. Perhaps we no longer belonged in the same circle of friends. Our employer may no longer have wanted us. Our position in the community was lost. Our sense of belonging had slipped away.

As a result, we may be impatient in our recovery. We may grasp for a place to belong, a place where we feel wanted and needed, a place where we can be accepted as we are.

Yet we must practice patience. Our Higher Power knows of such a place for us. When we are ready, we will be shown that place, and we will experience belonging and serenity. We do not know when we will arrive at this place, but it awaits us.

Do I remind myself today that there is a place where I belong?

THOUGHT FOR THE DAY

With patience and faith, I can and will belong.

INSPIRATION

At one time, most of us could not imagine having any kind of life with a mental illness. We wondered how someone with an illness like ours could possibly manage the illness, how someone could actually be happy, productive, and successful.

But as time passed and we saw others living successful lives, we found inspiration and hope. We began to believe it could happen to us. Now when we see others succeed, our inspiration is renewed and so is our belief in ourselves.

Today, do I believe that I, too, can succeed?

THOUGHT FOR THE DAY

*Let me recognize and appreciate the success
of other people with mental illness.*

CUTTING OURSELVES SOME SLACK

A woman with a mental illness asked a friend to scold her if she did one more thing wrong that day. Her friend replied, "No. I'm not going to scold you. You're doing a better job than I ever could."

The woman's friend was right. Many of us with a mental illness don't cut ourselves any slack. We may do so for others, but we punish ourselves for making the same mistakes.

We have a choice. We can continue to punish ourselves for being human and making mistakes, or we can begin forgiving ourselves, just as others do.

Do I cut myself some slack today?

THOUGHT FOR THE DAY

Forgiveness is a virtue.
Let me take responsibility for my actions,
but let me also lovingly forgive myself
just as much as I forgive others.

FEBRUARY

SELECTIVE LISTENING

Knowingly or not, some of us with a mental illness have developed selective listening. We hear what we want to hear and sometimes twist others' words to match our desires. For example, if we were told that we would have to take our medication for a long time, we interpreted that to mean we would be able to stop taking it whenever we felt a little better. Selective listening may give us some short-term comfort, but in the long-term it is dangerous.

As our recovery progresses, we need to learn to listen to what people say to us, not to what we want them to say. This may be difficult at first. Truth and reality can be painful. But our recovery will go nowhere if we base it on anything other than the truth.

Do I practice selective listening today or do I listen with an open heart and mind?

THOUGHT FOR THE DAY

As painful as it may be,
the truth always supports my recovery.

H.A.L.T.

When we find ourselves too hungry, too angry, too lonely, or too tired, we put ourselves at physical, emotional, or spiritual risk. Our body's chemistry changes and we can lose our balance.

For someone with a mental illness, this can have serious consequences. We need to restore our balance.

When we are hungry, we can eat. When we're angry, we can ask ourselves why, cope, and, if necessary, make a change. When we're lonely, we can reach out to others. When we're tired, we can rest.

Do I take care of myself today when I am hungry, angry, lonely, or tired?

THOUGHT FOR THE DAY

H.A.L.T. is the formula for balance.

NO MATTER WHAT, WE'LL BE OKAY

If we remember nothing else from our journey thus far, let us always remember in our hearts that, no matter what, we will be okay. That no matter where we may fall, or how often, we'll be okay. That no matter how many times we may have to start over, we'll be okay. That no matter what material possessions or amount of money we may lose, we'll be okay.

We may not have what we would like or what we think we should have, but we'll be okay because we have another chance. And most importantly, we still have our Higher Power and we have ourselves.

Today, do I know that, no matter what, I'll be okay?

THOUGHT FOR THE DAY

When I remain true to my Higher Power and to myself, I will always be okay, no matter what.

EACH DAY A NEW LESSON

Each day is a new step on our journey, with new lessons to be learned. Lessons for emotional and spiritual growth. Lessons in moral character. Lessons that lead us to acceptance and teach us that judging ourselves and others is not our job, but the work of our Higher Power. Lessons that teach us about our illness, help us heal, and help us cope with our illness, one day at a time.

Today, am I willing to learn any lessons that are given to me?

THOUGHT FOR THE DAY

*Let me learn the lessons of today
so I am prepared for tomorrow.*

SEEKING SOBRIETY

For most of us with mental illness, using street drugs or alcohol puts our spiritual, emotional, and physical health at risk. This is especially true for those of us in recovery from addiction or taking medication for our illness.

When we mix alcohol or other drugs with medications, we create a serious imbalance in our physical and emotional condition. This imbalance can cause irreversible damage to ourselves or others.

It's quite simple: If we continue to use, we are flirting with disaster and risking our most precious gift, the gift of life.

Am I drug- and alcohol-free today?

THOUGHT FOR THE DAY

*Sobriety can do far more for my journey ahead
than alcohol or other drugs can do for me today.*

LETTING GO

Those of us with a mental illness know better than anyone how little control we really have over our lives. We've also learned that with trust in a Power greater than ourselves, our life can have order and there is a plan for each of us. With trust in our Higher Power, we can let go, and letting go strengthens our faith that our lives have a purpose.

Let us have faith and follow the direction our Higher Power has set for us.

Am I willing to follow my Higher Power's direction today?

THOUGHT FOR THE DAY

*Faith means letting go and trusting
there's a Power greater than myself.*

PATIENT PROGRESS

Many of us experience impatience. We want to leap from no work to full-time work, from not being in a relationship to getting married, from knowing little about our illness to having all the answers.

But recovery is a step-by-step journey. It helps if we can take life one stage at a time and build solid foundations.

Am I impatient today or do I remember to live one step, one day at a time?

THOUGHT FOR THE DAY

Long-lasting change takes time.

FIGHTING WITH MYSELF

For many of us the shame and denial that come with mental illness have kept us from discovering who we are. We wished our illness would simply fade away. Yet fighting only builds barriers against self-acceptance.

We are blessed with a choice today: we can continue to fight or we can accept our illness for what it is. We can accept ourselves for who we are.

Today, can I stop fighting with myself and my illness and move on to acceptance and serenity?

THOUGHT FOR THE DAY

When I stop fighting I begin accepting.

AN UNFOLDING STORY

Our lives are like a story told one day at a time. Some of our story has been revealed; much remains. Yet life is not like a book in which you can skip ahead; life unfolds one day at a time.

Though it may be hard right now, let's not wish any of it away but live each day fully. We are the only ones who can write our story.

Am I fully present in my life today?

THOUGHT FOR THE DAY

*Change is not visible on a daily basis
but may be revealed when I am not looking.*

DOING SOMETHING PHYSICAL

Physical activity is important for those of us who have a mental illness. Whatever we can do is okay—walking, running, biking, yoga, or competitive sports—as long as it's physical. We will feel better for doing it.

We can exercise once a week, twice a week, or as often as we can. But the important thing is to start.

Do I include some physical activity in my recovery today?

THOUGHT FOR THE DAY

Taking care of my mind means taking care of my body.

CHANGING OUR BEHAVIOR

Any time we begin to change some aspect of our behavior, we experience resistance and question our motives. But our motives are simple: illness dictates change.

With illness, we must take good care of ourselves. We must become selfish and put our recovery first.

But changing behavior and learning to avoid old ways is a process. It takes patience, gentleness, and persistence. Chances are good we will take two steps forward and one step back. But with the help of our Higher Power, we can change our behavior— one day at a time.

Today, am I willing to change my behavior in healthy ways?

THOUGHT FOR THE DAY

Recovery means change.

• FEBRUARY 12 •

No Excuses

Having a mental illness is not an excuse for letting our lives slip away. Nor is it an excuse to avoid taking responsibility for our actions. Most of us, most of the time, are capable of managing our illness and conducting ourselves in a responsible manner.

But some of us use our mental illness as an excuse to give up on our goals, our dreams, ourselves. Because we have an illness, we deem ourselves unworthy, useless. We refuse to take responsibility for ourselves or our actions.

Coping with any mental illness takes tremendous courage and honesty. This includes challenging our excuses and carrying out our responsibilities. We move forward despite the illness.

Do I use excuses to hide from my life today or do I continue forward, one day at a time?

Thought for the Day

Excuses hold me back from leading a fulfilling life.

WHEN TO GET HELP

The most significant lesson we can learn is when to check in. In other words, when to get help.

Starting today, let us make or renew our commitment to be alert for the warning signs of our illness. That way, we will know intuitively when we need to check in.

Do I practice learning the warning signs—and check in today if necessary?

THOUGHT FOR THE DAY

I know what it feels like to want to check out.
All the more reason to learn to check in.

SAVED BY LOVE

Many of us disliked or even hated ourselves for the harm our illness caused us and others. Perhaps we felt it had made us unworthy and that we were destined for a life of loneliness. How could anyone love someone who was mentally ill?

Yet we all deserve to be loved, and we all have the chance to give and receive love. Love can save us if we are willing and able to love ourselves, if we can let others love us, and if we trust that our Higher Power accepts us unconditionally.

Let us open our hearts and begin forgiving ourselves, so that we too may be saved by love.

Do I practice loving myself and letting others love me today?

THOUGHT FOR THE DAY

Love can heal when I allow it to reach me.

MEMORY LOSS

Many of us with mental illness have memory problems. Sometimes it's due to our medication or other treatments. Whatever the cause, our memory is not what it used to be and we get frustrated and angry. *Why us? What can we do about it?*

Whether permanent or temporary, we can cope with this loss by writing things down and leaving ourselves reminders. We can also develop a sense of humor. Perhaps we can forget how often we don't remember.

If I have trouble remembering things today, do I write reminders and go easy on myself?

THOUGHT FOR THE DAY

My life can still be meaningful and productive with occasional memory loss.

THE PROBLEM WITH PERFECTIONISM

We all have shortcomings. Yet many of us strive for perfection. And when we fail to reach it, we feel ashamed. We lose our sense of progress.

Shortcomings are part of human nature. Demanding perfection of ourselves will not make us who we *think* we ought to be. It will only stop us from becoming who we *truly* are.

Do I accept myself and my shortcomings today?

THOUGHT FOR THE DAY

*I will move forward with courage, hope, and patience—
and without trying to be perfect.*

ANGER

We all get angry at times. We get angry at ourselves, other people, our illness, our Higher Power, and so on. In most cases it's healthy to express a little anger, as long as it's done appropriately. But we must watch out for the level of anger. We do not want our anger to turn into rage so that we harm ourselves or others.

Coping with anger can be done by talking to ourselves and others about why we're angry, by journaling, and by turning things over to our Higher Power.

Do I cope appropriately with my anger today?

THOUGHT FOR THE DAY

Anger is a normal feeling.
What matters is how I express it.

Sanity Can Be Restored

We can remember just how insane our lives had become when our illness controlled us. We lost control emotionally and were driven to despair. Or a barrage of voices was telling us what to do. We wondered whether we would ever feel sane again. But sanity is relative, and it is different for each of us with a mental illness.

Whatever sanity is for us, let us remember that it can be restored. But it can be done only one day at a time.

Today, have I done what I can to cope with my illness and maintain or restore my sanity?

Thought for the Day

I move toward sanity step by step.

SEX AND SERENITY

Many of us with mental illness are far from content with our sexuality or sex lives. Perhaps our medication has changed our ability to be emotionally and physically intimate. Perhaps we have too little or too much sex. Perhaps we are embarrassed and confused about the whole situation.

Yet, over time, we can gain understanding and self-acceptance. By remaining honest with ourselves and our Higher Power about our feelings, we can find balance and serenity when it comes to sex.

Do I seek a healthy balance regarding sex today?

THOUGHT FOR THE DAY

Honesty and soul-searching can help me develop a healthy outlook on my sexuality.

HOME AFTER TREATMENT

Many of us with a mental illness have had inpatient treatment. On returning home, we felt anxious. Home may no longer have felt safe. Perhaps others had taken on our role. Perhaps our loved ones treated us differently. Or the familiar now seemed unfamiliar. In short, our home had changed.

Returning home can be an adjustment. It means learning to express our thoughts and feelings more clearly, learning to ask for help, and learning to set new boundaries. It also means helping family members, friends, or partners adjust to having us back home.

Today, do I do my part in making the adjustment?

THOUGHT FOR THE DAY

*Despite the changes, I can find a new way
of being with others I care about.*

THE NEXT STEP

All that is required of us today is to put one foot in front of the other and do the best we can, one thing at a time, one step at a time.

It helps if we don't try to do too many things at once or do them too fast. That way, we won't miss out on the miracles that can happen throughout the day.

Today, let us take it one step at a time and look for miracles.

Do I take today one step at a time?

THOUGHT FOR THE DAY

It's much easier and less stressful to take things one step at a time.

Accepting Help from Others

Accepting the help of others is a dilemma for many of us. We are often embarrassed by our illness and want to shy away from others.

Yet when we come to accept ourselves and our illness, we can see that everybody needs a helping hand now and then. We see that others want to help us because they care about us. Then our embarrassment subsides and we can begin to accept the help that we need and deserve.

Do I let others help me today?

Thought for the Day

Accepting help in a time of need
means I won't feel lost and hopeless.

THIS TOO SHALL PASS

Whether we are just beginning our recovery or have been coping with our illness for some time, we may find ourselves at wit's end, believing that everything is hopeless and that our life will never improve.

When we begin to feel this way, let us first remember that *this too shall pass*. In ten minutes, thirty minutes, an hour, or a day, things can change. That feeling of hopelessness can fade.

Today, do I believe that this too shall pass?

THOUGHT FOR THE DAY

Whatever may be troubling me right now,
this too shall pass.

IT TAKES COURAGE

There is no question that it takes courage to cope with mental illness day after day. It takes courage to face the risks. It takes courage to be honest with ourselves and others about our illness and how we feel. And it takes courage to rebound after a setback or relapse.

Yet every one of us has this courage inside, if only we would look for it and ask our Higher Power to help us see it.

Today, let us walk forward on our journey with courage.

Have I found the courage I need to cope with my life and my illness today?

THOUGHT FOR THE DAY

Courage begins within and turns into action.

OUR PURPOSE AND VALUE

Our illness held us prisoner for long periods of time. Perhaps we concluded that years of our lives were wasted.

They weren't. Years of coping prepared us for today and for the journey ahead. That experience can help us to help ourselves and others we may meet, now and in the future. Each of us has a purpose here on Earth.

Can I see the value and purpose in my life today?

THOUGHT FOR THE DAY

What I may dismiss as valueless
may someday turn out to be very valuable indeed.

FEAR OF CHANGE

Each day we are granted a new chance to make change: to accept ourselves and our illness, to grow, to help others.

But change brings on fear. And fear brings on resistance. If we fear too much, nothing will change and we won't move forward.

Can I practice making changes today *alongside* my fear?

THOUGHT FOR THE DAY

It is only through change that healing occurs.

A DIAGNOSIS MEANS HOPE

When we were first diagnosed with a mental illness, our waiting and wondering were over. Finally we had an explanation for what we had felt and done, for what had happened to us.

This diagnosis did not make our past less painful, but it was a ray of hope. Why? Because naming the problem is the first step toward finding a solution, a first step toward understanding and acceptance.

Today, do I see how my diagnosis is a source of hope?

THOUGHT FOR THE DAY

When I face the reality of my illness,
I can begin my journey of recovery.

AMENDS

When our illness took control of our lives, our behavior was out of control for a time. It led us down a road that hurt ourselves and others.

But in recovery there is a solution for dealing with that powerlessness: assess the damage we did to ourselves and others, make peace, and make what amends we can. We can then begin moving forward again with our lives and our recovery.

Today, have I made peace with myself and others for the damage that I have caused, and made what amends I can?

THOUGHT FOR THE DAY

Whether healthy or ill, I am responsible for my actions.

WE ARE WHO WE ARE

With its painful smptoms and unpredictability, it is difficult to keep accepting our illness. It can become quite easy to fall into a pattern of wanting to be someone else.

But we are who we are. Wishing, pleading, and demanding will not change this. We cannot be someone else, no matter how hard we try.

For today, do I truly accept who I am?

THOUGHT FOR THE DAY

I can only be myself.

MARCH

Getting to Know Our Illness

Though it may fade from time to time, our illness will likely be with us for some time. With it come pain, loneliness, and uncertainty. At times it is overwhelming.

As much as we wish the illness gone, it helps to pay attention to it so we can learn from it. Over time, we will come to accept it and find more ways to cope.

Am I in denial today or am I coming to know my illness and its symptoms?

Thought for the Day

My illness can teach me how to take care of myself.

Supporting Others with Mental Illness

Those of us with mental illness have a responsibility to reach out and help those who will accept our help. We humbly give of ourselves. We bear witness to those who are not as fortunate as we are. We share our experience, strength, and hope. We do not play God nor do we claim responsibility for any success. We do this because by helping others, we're helping ourselves.

Am I willing to help someone with a mental illness today?

Thought for the Day

To keep what I have been given, I must give it away.

First Things First

How wonderful to be excited in recovery and filled with hope. We look forward to taking back our lives. To do that we need to address our emotional, physical, and spiritual health. We must get as emotionally grounded as possible and stay as physically fit as we can. Spiritually, we keep in touch with our Higher Power. This is our foundation from which we grow.

Do I put first things first in my recovery today?

Thought for the Day

To build anything requires a solid foundation.

GIVING AWAY OUR GIFTS

Just as others have shared their knowledge and wisdom with us, we can share ourselves with others in turn. When the time comes, we need to pass along what has been given to us—for the sake of others and for ourselves.

If we hoard those gifts, they will lose some value and purpose. But if we give them away, they will come back in ways we cannot imagine.

Do I share my knowledge and wisdom with others today?

THOUGHT FOR THE DAY

To keep the gifts I have been given,
I share them with others.

Tug of War

Many of us are caught in an emotional and spiritual tug of war between fear and faith, belief and unbelief, trust and mistrust. It is a tug of war between our past, present, and future.

But with the guidance of our Higher Power and others who understand, we can survive this tug of war and attain acceptance and serenity. However, this can only be done one day at a time.

Today, do I remind myself that there is a Power greater than what I am feeling right now?

Thought for the Day

There are still times of emotional upheaval in recovery but I now know what I have to do to get through them.

NO ONE SAID IT WOULD BE EASY

Coping with a mental illness is anything but easy. It is not easy to live with its limitations. It is not easy to feel positive and stable one day and down and out of control the next. And it is certainly not easy to accept that our illness may remain part of us for some time to come.

But no one ever said it would be easy.

Despite the challenges, do I move forward today with courage, compassion, and patience?

THOUGHT FOR THE DAY

When coping with my illness seems too difficult—
or even life itself seems unbearable—I simply do my best.

DOING OUR PART

We have a mental illness. To stay as healthy as possible, we need help from our Higher Power and others.

But we must be willing to do our part, to take responsibility for ourselves. We need to become as healthy as we can—emotionally, physically, and spiritually.

Do I do what I can to stay healthy today?

THOUGHT FOR THE DAY

*When I take responsibility for managing
my illness, I am on my way to serenity
and have the best chance of recovery.*

THE RIGHT ATTITUDE

We can choose our attitude and our expectations. We can go about our day consumed with anger, self-pity, and resentment, and make all our decisions based on fear.

Or we can choose to reach deep within and discover an outlook governed by hope and vision, driven by peace and acceptance of ourselves and others, an outlook of gratitude rather than self-indulgence and self-pity.

What is my attitude today?

THOUGHT FOR THE DAY

The right attitude points me in the right direction.

MAINTAINING SELF–ESTEEM

Those of us with a mental illness know that when our illness is active, it can take away our self-esteem. It can also leave us feeling as if we cannot do our job, be close to our friends and families, or take care of everyday things in our lives.

When we feel our self-esteem slipping away, it is time to reach out for help. Others can help bring us back to reality with positive messages. As our recovery progresses, we will learn how to give ourselves positive messages.

Am I doing what I can to maintain my self-esteem today?

THOUGHT FOR THE DAY

Reaching out to others helps maintain self-esteem.

BEING UNDERSTOOD

We may think at times that we are the only ones who have a mental illness and that no one else could possibly understand who we are and what we have endured.

But the truth is that many other people have been hospitalized or take medications for psychiatric reasons; many others have had the same feelings we have had. They understand and would be willing to share themselves with us if we just asked them and allowed them to help. We need not be ashamed or embarrassed about who we are or what we have done.

Let us have faith and reach out to others.

Today, do I know, deep in my heart, that there are others who understand me?

THOUGHT FOR THE DAY

When others understand me, I no longer walk alone.

THE IMPORTANCE OF FAITH

Over time, we will come to accept ourselves and our illness, as others have. But it helps to have faith in ourselves and our Higher Power. Even if we think our Higher Power has left our side, rest assured that this Power is with us. And when we stay close to our Higher Power, miracles can happen.

Today, do I realize that my Higher Power is beside me, guiding me, every day and in every breath?

THOUGHT FOR THE DAY

Faith and trust in myself go hand-in-hand
with faith and trust in my Higher Power.

PEOPLE-PLEASING

For some of us, people-pleasing has become a way of getting our needs and wants met. But people-pleasing is manipulative and condescending. And it cheats us. When we are busy pleasing others, we are not being true to ourselves (nor those we are pleasing).

Rather than manipulating people, let us simply ask for what we need and want. We are all lovable and deserving, just as we are. We can truly please ourselves and others by simply being ourselves.

Do I ask honestly for what I want or need today?

THOUGHT FOR THE DAY

The path to true connection is to be myself.
The path to getting what I need is to ask for it.

I Am Who I Am

Sometimes we want to be someone else—anyone but who we are. We want to be someone who doesn't have a mental illness, someone who feels more free and at peace. We want to be someone who doesn't have to take medications day after day. We want to be free of the pain and loneliness our illness has brought us.

But whether we get what we want or not, what we *need* is to accept ourselves, our illness, a desire to become well, and the guidance of our Higher Power.

Today, do I accept myself, my illness, and the guidance of my Higher Power? Do I commit myself to recovery?

Thought for the Day

When I look within, I will discover that accepting myself and being myself are far more fulfilling than expected.

HIGHER POWER PROMISES

Our Higher Power promises to take us to that place where we truly belong and feel free. A place where peace is abundant and natural, where we can help and comfort others like ourselves.

In return, we promise to remain patient, trust in ourselves, and trust especially in the steadfastness and direction of our Higher Power.

Do I trust that my Higher Power will guide me on my journey today and every day?

THOUGHT FOR THE DAY

*Recovery requires commitment
to a Power greater than myself.*

DOING WHAT IS GOOD FOR US

In the process of managing our illness, doctors, nurses, family, and friends will surely have many recommendations for us. Some we won't like. But some we need to follow just the same.

Some of the things that are good for us are the hardest to do. But if we ask ourselves *Is this good for me?* and the answer is yes, then chances are we need to do it. Our efforts will likely be rewarded.

Do I do what is best for my recovery today, even if I don't want to?

THOUGHT FOR THE DAY

Recovery means change; recovery means work.

TAKING MEDICATIONS DAILY

Many of us take medications on a daily basis. We do so to make sure that we stay healthy emotionally, physically, and spiritually.

We need to remind ourselves that taking our medications is a sign of self-esteem and courage rather than shame and weakness of character.

Today, can I feel good about myself when I take my medications knowing that this action supports my health?

THOUGHT FOR THE DAY

I take my medications because I care about myself.

THE PROBLEM WITH SECRETS

Secrets add to our burden of guilt and shame. They drive us toward isolation. They keep us stuck and sick until we release them.

Today, little by little, we can begin revealing to others we trust what has been festering in our souls. With each secret we reveal, we take back a part of our lives. But we must begin with the first step and the first secret.

Can I share at least one of my secrets today with someone I trust?

THOUGHT FOR THE DAY

Revealing my secrets to people I trust makes me healthier.

FOLLOWING OUR HEARTS

Everyone has moments of self-doubt, but there are many more for those of us with mental illness. We question our ability to decide or judge.

As a result, we may have learned not to trust our own thoughts and feelings. But just as we learned not to trust ourselves, we can learn to trust again. With time and practice, we can relearn to follow our hearts fearlessly.

Can I begin to trust my own heart today?

THOUGHT FOR THE DAY

With recovery comes the return of self-confidence.

MAKING DECISIONS

In recovery from a mental illness, we may find ourselves in many challenging situations that require difficult decisions. These situations may require patience and deliberation before taking the next step. Some decisions could have serious and long-standing effects on our lives and the lives of others.

When coping with our illness, let us strive to make healthy and wise decisions so we do not put ourselves or others in danger.

Am I patient and deliberate today as I make decisions?

THOUGHT FOR THE DAY

*Let me always think and consult my heart
before I decide.*

• MARCH 20 •

NEW WAYS TO MANAGE OUR ILLNESS

Learning to cope with and manage the symptoms of our illness is most likely a lifelong process. What has worked for us in one situation may not work for us in another. What has worked in the past, may not work in the future. Our illness, its symptoms, and the effects of our medications can all change— sometimes rapidly.

New situations are an opportunity to learn and relearn ways to cope with and manage our illness. We need an open mind and the willingness to adjust. If we lose the willingness to learn and change, our illness will manage us.

Am I open to new ways of managing my illness today?

THOUGHT FOR THE DAY

When old ways fail, I will seek new options.

Is This Healthy for Me?

We must not get too discouraged when we find ourselves in need or when our old instincts give us familiar but harmful advice. We can just set aside our old ways and work on developing new instincts instead.

But don't completely discard these old instincts for they may still be of help. They remind us what *not* to do. When confronted with them, a useful technique is to ask ourselves, *Is this healthy for me?* If we are not sure, we can ask someone who cares about us, someone we trust.

Today, do I let go of harmful instincts and work on developing helpful ones?

Thought for the Day

My past is a good teacher.

REJOINING COMMUNITY

Most of us know what it is like to be part of a community. But we may have lost our community when our illness took control of our lives.

As we begin feeling better, most of us can return to our communities. But it will likely take time to recover and become the fully functioning members we want to be.

Today, let us be patient and allow healing to take place.

THOUGHT FOR THE DAY

With recovery I find my place in my community.

CREATING A SPIRITUAL LIFE

Just as we are on a journey of coping and healing, we are also on a journey of finding or rebuilding our spiritual life.

We begin by trusting something greater than ourselves, a Higher Power that will guide us on our journey, a Higher Power we can depend on minute by minute, hour by hour, and day by day. We can experience this Higher Power both by looking within and by looking for support without.

Today, am I building a spiritual life?

THOUGHT FOR THE DAY

Spirituality begins with trust.

CHANGE AND GROWTH

Our lives will change whether we want them to or not. Change is guaranteed but growth is optional.

To grow, we need to accept change. To grow, we need to learn from change.

Recovery means change. Change usually brings on resistance. It's not easy, but if we can accept change and learn from it, we will grow and recover.

Today, can I let go of my resistance to change?

THOUGHT FOR THE DAY

Change is an opportunity for growth.

Victims or Survivors?

We can allow ourselves to become victims of our illness or we can become survivors. We can continually feel sorry for ourselves—living lives consumed with self-pity, anger, and resentment—or we can grow. We can stay stuck or begin recovery.

Transformation is not without some fear, sacrifice, and uncertainty. But the rewards of being a survivor far outweigh those of being a victim.

Today, do I think of myself as a victim or as a survivor?

Thought for the Day

As a victim, I am powerless.
As a survivor, I am empowered.

• MARCH 26 •

WHY?

Sometimes on our journey we may pause and wonder why: Why are we the ones with mental illness? Why have our lives turned out the way they have? Why can't they be the way we want them to be?

Chances are, few or no answers appear. Before we can move forward, we first must learn to simply accept what has happened rather than continue to question. This is the first step to serenity.

Today, can I practice accepting what I cannot change?

THOUGHT FOR THE DAY

Learning to accept brings about clarity and serenity.

JUDGING OURSELVES

Many of us declare ourselves guilty of all kinds of sins. We tell ourselves that we are no longer worthy and sentence ourselves to guilt, shame, and isolation.

But we do not have to.

On our journey we will make mistakes. But rather than condemn ourselves, let us learn from our mistakes.

Do I judge myself harshly for my actions today, or do I let myself be human?

THOUGHT FOR THE DAY

Rather than sentence myself to misery,
I can humbly learn from my mistakes.

READY OR NOT

On our journey, we will have new opportunities and face new challenges. Some we will be ready for and meet with enthusiasm. With others, fear and self-doubt will hold us back.

Recovery is built on progress not perfection. It helps to be patient and gentle with ourselves. When we are ready, we will walk. When ready, we will take one opportunity or challenge at a time.

Today, do I recognize when I am ready and when to wait for another time?

THOUGHT FOR THE DAY

Wisdom is knowing when to act and when to wait.

QUIET TIME

Regular quiet time is a must for those of us with a mental illness. Our physical, emotional, and spiritual health depend on it. We need to give ourselves a chance to get centered: to restore our energy, gather our thoughts, and just relax. Rather than demand more of ourselves than we can give, we need to stop, breathe, and be silent for a while.

Quiet time is an essential part of our recovery. It enables us to stay in touch with ourselves and our Higher Power.

Do I take some quiet time for myself today?

THOUGHT FOR THE DAY

Quiet time is essential for my mental health.

THE POSSIBILITY OF PEACE

The possibility of peace and contentment lies within each of us. No matter how far down we may go, or what our situation may be today, peace and contentment are possible.

We do not have to live in the fear and loneliness that our illness has shown us many times. We do not have to face each day with the familiar feelings of inadequacy that our illness can project upon us. We do not have to live in constant fear of the present and the future.

But just how does this transformation to a place of peace happen? It happens gradually, through faith, hope, and acceptance. It happens through our triumphs and struggles, our questioning and understanding. In essence, we get there by living life one day at a time.

Have I discovered the possibility of peace that lies within me today?

THOUGHT FOR THE DAY

Faith, hope, and acceptance are keys to peace and contentment.

❈

AFFIRMATIONS—ANYTIME, ANYWHERE

When we write affirmations or speak them out loud, we declare—and begin to create—what we want in our lives. Whether about healing, creating a spiritual bond, or changing a negative to a positive, affirmations are tools we can use anytime and anywhere.

When our day-to-day frustrations and setbacks cause us to doubt our abilities or self-worth, we may need a reminder about who we are. Affirmations give us these reminders. For example, *My life has meaning and a purpose.* Or, *I can cope with my illness today.* Or, *I can be gentle with myself.* Or, *I can ask for help and not be embarrassed.* We can create an affirmation to meet any need.

Do I choose to stay stuck in self-doubt and negativity or do I affirm my life today?

THOUGHT FOR THE DAY

*Affirmations are always available
and can help me change and heal.*

❋

APRIL

FRIENDS LIKE US

There are people who know all about us and our illness. They are just like us. They have traveled their own journeys with their own illnesses, and truly understand what we are going through. They can't take away our illness just by offering friendship or understanding, but they can empathize with our frustration and hopelessness as we cope with the unknowns of our illness. These friends can also support us in our belief that we will be able to manage our illness and begin taking back our life. They can offer hope to carry us through the hard times.

Today, do I remember that there are others like me—people who understand and care?

THOUGHT FOR THE DAY

Others have made journeys like mine and they will support me if I just reach out.

AVOIDING SELF-DESTRUCTION

It isn't that we want to ruin our lives, but many of us with mental illness haven't learned how to cope with our feelings and situations. We may deal with them in ways that only make our lives more difficult.

Eventually, however, we begin to see the consequences of such behavior. And we begin to see that we can also unlearn it.

If all is not going well in our lives, we don't have to be self-destructive any longer. We can start getting help—from friends and professionals and our Higher Power. Changes never happen as fast as we'd like, but change will come eventually if we do our part.

Today, do I seek out healthy alternatives to my self-defeating behaviors?

THOUGHT FOR THE DAY

When I seek out healthy alternatives,
I will find support.

TAKING BACK OUR LIVES

Most of us have had big parts of our lives taken away. We lost hopes, dreams, and for a time, perhaps ourselves.

But today, many of us can say that we have begun taking back our lives. We have begun the healing journey and reclaiming what we had lost.

Today, we are no longer prisoners of our illness. We have learned to accept ourselves and our illness. We have learned that taking back our life demands commitment, willingness, tolerance, and above all, patience. It is a lifelong journey. But now we know it can be done and that it is a journey well worth taking.

Am I taking back my life today?

THOUGHT FOR THE DAY

With the help of my Higher Power
I can take back my life, one day at a time

❋

• A P R I L 4 •

WHAT LIES WITHIN US

What lies in our past and what lies before us are nothing compared to what lies within us at this very moment. Yet many of us choose to focus on the past or future—and thus overlook this moment and ourselves.

We cannot live in the past because it is gone. We cannot live in the future because it does not exist. All we have is today and what lies within us. Let us live fully by being present in this and every moment.

Am I stuck in memories of the past or thoughts of the future? Or can I discover what lies within me today?

THOUGHT FOR THE DAY

I can stop running from myself and live in the present.

KEEPING IT SIMPLE

We will have days when every thought, feeling, and action seem to fade into madness. Self-doubt, self-pity, anger, and hopelessness consume us. Rational thinking is difficult.

On those days we keep things as simple as we can. We think only about the here and now, what is taking place this very minute. We limit our obsessive thoughts as best we can. We do not dwell on the negative whispering in our minds. We remind ourselves that we can't handle everything at once.

Do I know when and how to keep my life simple? Is today one of those days?

THOUGHT FOR THE DAY

I can simplify my life.

IMPATIENT FOR DIRECTION

Many of us want answers about our new direction. Our lives pose difficult questions and we expect clear answers immediately.

Yet we must remain patient. Our direction and answers are not always revealed on our time table. But when the time is right, we will know.

Can I relax, remain patient, and let my Higher Power run my life today?

THOUGHT FOR THE DAY

I will find my direction if I am patient
and open to guidance from my Higher Power
and the people I trust.

LOVING MYSELF

The ultimate goals of recovery are to love ourselves as we are and to have serenity in our lives. With a mental illness, this can be difficult. But the first step is simple.

We need not believe our illness when it tells us that we are unworthy of love and thus unable to love ourselves or receive love from our Higher Power. Instead, we can remind ourselves that we are worthy and lovable, that our Higher Power accepts us just as we are and can be trusted to guide us on our journey. The more we practice such thinking, the more we will come to accept it, and the more serenity we will have.

Do I love myself just as I am today?

THOUGHT FOR THE DAY

Loving myself, in spite of my illness and my defects, leads to serenity.

✳

SABOTAGE

Thoughts of suicide may be common among those of us with mental illness. So is acting on them. Many people have lost their lives when what began as a thought turned into a compulsion that was eventually acted upon.

But just as fast as our suicidal thoughts begin, we can learn to disable them. We can interrupt our thought process before it becomes a compulsion. To start, we can confront, cope with, or remove ourselves from our situation. Then we can turn to someone for help. It may take practice and patience, but we can learn to do it.

If I entertain thoughts of suicide today, can I disable them before they become a compulsion?

THOUGHT FOR THE DAY

With practice, I can avoid compulsive action
and seek help.

SCARS

We have all endured a great deal of pain and have the emotional and spiritual scars to prove it. We need not be embarrassed or ashamed about these scars. Nor should we boast about them or try to make ourselves out to be heroes.

It is through a Power greater than ourselves that we are here today. Our scars remind us just where we come from. They remind us to help and share with others.

Do I use my experience to learn, grow, and help others today?

THOUGHT FOR THE DAY

Behind my scars can be wisdom
with which I can help myself and others.

HELPING OTHERS

Sometimes when our illness takes control, it's all we can do to take care of ourselves. But when we're feeling well, we can give back a little of what we have received. We can volunteer with the local branch of the National Alliance of the Mentally Ill. We can visit others who have a mental illness. We can be present at support group meetings.

What can I do today to help others with mental illness?

THOUGHT FOR THE DAY

Helping others when I am able,
makes me even stronger.

DIRECT AND HONEST

When it comes to coping with a mental illness, we cannot afford to be anything but direct and honest with ourselves and others. We cannot tell half-truths about how we are feeling or avoid asking for what we need. People may be uncomfortable with this, but for our safety and sanity, it is a must.

This is not a game of Truth or Dare. It is about setting boundaries with ourselves and others, and living by them as best we can. It is about protecting and preserving our life and all that we have worked so hard for.

Today, am I direct and honest with others—and with myself?

THOUGHT FOR THE DAY

*Being direct and honest helps me
to live more fully and serenely.*

A Long-Term Commitment

As days pass and we face fewer issues, do we grow complacent? Do we begin to believe that we are cured and that our illness no longer needs attention and guidance?

Living with mental illness requires that we do our best to protect our sanity. We put our emotional, physical, and spiritual health above all else. Whether we feel well or ill, it is critical that we take care of ourselves by monitoring ourselves and taking the correct medications.

Do I commit myself fully to recovery today?

Thought for the Day

My health and recovery must always come first, and my commitment must be wholehearted.

No Need for Embarrassment

Whether it's for therapy or a medication check, we likely will need to go to a mental health clinic or counselor. For many of us, the waiting room is not comfortable. We feel exposed. Everyone knows we have a mental illness or we wouldn't be there.

And yet, why the fuss? All of us are there for the same reason. We want to get healthy and stay healthy. There, we are more alike than different.

Do I feel embarrassed when I see the doctor or counselor for my illness? Do I feel grateful for the help today?

Thought for the Day

*I will no longer be embarrassed
when I have fully accepted myself and my illness.*

WISDOM AWAITS

Sometimes we get so caught up with the events in our lives that we overlook the wisdom to be gained from them. We feel overwhelmed and prefer to forget.

Yet experience can be a great teacher. With our illness and our unique symptoms, we need all the wisdom we can get.

Today, do I pause to reflect on my day and see what I can learn?

THOUGHT FOR THE DAY

If I pay attention, I can learn from all my experiences.

LYING LOW

Some days we know intuitively that trying to face the day ahead could be more harmful than doing nothing. As we get to know ourselves, our illness, and its symptoms, we learn when it is best to just lie low.

On those days we put our emotional, physical, and spiritual health above all else. We are gentle with ourselves until our symptoms pass. There is no shame in taking time for ourselves when we need to. It is part of the healing process, and it is up to us to practice.

Today, do I know when I need to lie low?

THOUGHT FOR THE DAY

There are times for motion and progress,
and times for being still and allowing healing within.

FINDING FELLOWSHIP

By now, most of us have discovered that we do not need to manage our illness alone. There are many others just like us who need us as much as we need them.

Finding fellowship with others who have a mental illness is just a phone call away. But if we are afraid and unwilling to reach out, fellowship may as well be a thousand miles away.

It is up to us to search out this fellowship. We can pick up the phone, send an e-mail, or search the Internet for a support group. We can take that all-important first step toward fellowship.

Today, do I reach out for the fellowship of others like me?

THOUGHT FOR THE DAY

The comfort of fellowship
is just on the other side of fear.

• A P R I L   1 7 •

CLIMBING THE LADDER

At one time or another, most of us have fallen off the ladder of life. We may have lost not only our sanity, but our self-respect, spirituality, material possessions, and even our sense of self. Our illness left us emotionally, physically, and spiritually bankrupt. For many of us, this is when we turned our lives around and began climbing back up the ladder of life.

As we do this, however, let us remember that it can only be done one step at a time. At times we may become impatient and feel we should have already reached the top. But climbing back up the ladder of life cannot be done in a giant leap. It is a process that takes time, patience, persistence, and faith. Climbing one step at a time, we can eventually regain our lives.

Do I let my impatience put me in danger of falling back to the bottom today or can I follow one step with another on the ladder of life?

THOUGHT FOR THE DAY

It is much easier to reach the top
when I take one step at a time.

❋

THE MEANING OF MEMORIES

When our illness first began, we spent much time reliving memories of what we were once able to do. These memories brought us both pleasure and grief: pleasure by helping us revisit people and events that we treasured, grief by reminding us of what we could no longer do or no longer become.

We relived these memories to feel more alive. Yet we also used them to help avoid the present. Over time, we began to feel that our life was empty and meaningless except for these memories. Over time, we could see that if we were to recover, we would need to find our way back to the present. And when we did, we discovered that, although we have an illness, the present is often far more rewarding than any memory.

Today, do I live in the past or in the present?

THOUGHT FOR THE DAY

Life is lived most fully in the present.

Too Much at Stake

There is too much at stake for us to take our recovery for granted. At times our illness can be predictable and easily managed. But at other times it can be unpredictable and even dangerous.

Therefore, when it comes to our physical, emotional, and spiritual health, we cannot afford to be complacent, even for a day. We cannot afford to be careless with our medication or allow ourselves to slip into a mental or emotional state that impairs our judgment. Nor can we afford to isolate ourselves, no matter how much we may want to. If we allow ourselves to take our recovery for granted, we risk losing what we have worked so hard to gain.

Do I realize just how much is at stake in my life today?

Thought for the Day

*Sometimes I don't realize the value
of what I have until I no longer have it.*

✦

WITH CONVICTION

Whatever we choose to do on our journey, we do it with all our heart. We do it with purity and conviction. We do it with love to help ourselves and others.

As we continue on our journey, let us have the courage to accept the guidance of our Higher Power, one day and one breath at a time.

Do I act with all my heart today?

THOUGHT FOR THE DAY

When my motives are pure and I act with all my heart,
I rise above my selfish impulses and desires.

• APRIL 21 •

JUST ENOUGH STRENGTH

Chances are, at some point in our lives some of us have felt like something in us was dying. We felt helpless, as if our soul had been taken away by our illness. Perhaps we lost our sense of self and believed we were past the point of no return.

Yet it often happens that we find we have just enough strength to reach out and seek help. Slowly, we begin to feel better. We get healthier. Slowly, we draw back from that point of no return. For this we are profoundly grateful.

Today, do I remember that no matter how I may feel right now, it is always possible to regain my life and reconnect with others and with my Higher Power?

THOUGHT FOR THE DAY

It is never too late to change.

KNOWING WHAT TO DO

Many of us have been hospitalized before, some of us from having attempted suicide. It's likely that we did not want to go in but our illness had control of us.

We may not need to go in again, but if we do, chances are we won't want to go in then either. But if it does happen, it can be different because of what we've learned. Now we can see when we need help and we know where to get it. We can go in voluntarily for our own well-being and safety.

Will I seek help today if I need it?

THOUGHT FOR THE DAY

It's a sign of health when I know what to do when I need help.

GUIDED THROUGH ANOTHER DAY

Each day when we awaken, let us remind ourselves that we will not be alone if we ask our Higher Power to guide us.

Some days we have hope and faith and patience and all goes well. But other days we are consumed with fear and impatience, and wonder just what's next for us.

But when we pray for help, by some miracle we are guided through the day and a new day with new opportunities soon follows.

Today, do I ask my Higher Power to give me strength and guide me through another day?

THOUGHT FOR THE DAY

No matter how badly a day is going,
there will be a new day soon.

✸

GETTING BACK UP

We will fall many times on our journey. Sometimes we fall sudden and hard. This is part of life for everyone, not just those of us with a mental illness.

So what do we do once we have fallen? Do we stay on the ground? Or do we get back up?

With courage and the help of our Higher Power, we can face whatever took us to the ground, get back up, and begin again.

If I fall today, can I get back up?

THOUGHT FOR THE DAY

*There is no shame when I fall
and much dignity and strength to be gained by getting up.*

• APRIL 25 •

BEING PRESENT

Reality can be a difficult place to live. Sometimes it seems impossible to stay in the here and now.

From time to time we all revisit the past and yearn for the future. This is natural. Being present every minute of the day is impossible for anyone.

Still, we can strive to be present for as many minutes as we can. We strive for progress, not perfection.

Today, am I doing what I can to be present?

THOUGHT FOR THE DAY

A small dose of reality is better than no reality at all.

Only Part of Us

There is no question that our illness is and should be at the center of our lives, but it doesn't have to become all of us. Just because we live with our illness twenty-four hours a day doesn't mean that's all we should talk or think about.

Granted, there are times in our recovery when we must focus entirely on managing and coping with our illness. But these times pass, and when they do, we can seize the opportunity to move beyond the boundaries of our illness.

Does my illness consume me today, or do I make use of the gifts and talents that were so graciously given to me?

Thought for the Day

Mental illness does not define me.

We Are Who We Think We Are

How we think about ourselves has an impact on what we do. If we decide that we are less of a person because we have a mental illness, then we may not fulfill our potential. If we decide our illness will consume our every thought and action for the rest of our lives, then it probably will. If we decide that we will always be a victim and our life will bring us nothing but misfortune, then our life may just turn out that way.

On the other hand, if we begin to believe positive things about ourselves, eventually our outlook on life will become positive as well. When we believe that we are lovable, that we can cope with our illness, and that we are no less of a person because of it, then this is what shall be. We can change who we are by changing who we believe ourselves to be.

Today, do I remind myself of my abilities, my choices, and my opportunities?

Thought for the Day

*My attitude and perspective can make life
more positive and joyful.*

❋

FOR FUN

Many of us can get so bogged down with our daily schedules, our responsibilities, and the seriousness of our illness that we neglect to have fun.

Now is the time to add fun back into our life. We can get out a baseball, football, Frisbee, golf clubs, or fishing rod. We can go out to dinner, take in a concert, or see a movie with friends.

We all need fun in our lives regardless of our situation or condition. And fun makes difficult journeys a bit easier.

Can I do something fun today?

THOUGHT FOR THE DAY

*Having fun is an important part
of my sanity and recovery.*

AVOIDING JUDGMENT

We have every right to hold our head high, for we have survived despair and we are taking back our lives. We have learned to live our lives and cope with our illness as best we can, each and every day. We have come to accept it as part of our life. To arrive at this point in our recovery, we have done what has been asked of us and more. We have grown a great deal.

If others suggest that our journey has not been so difficult, or that we are not doing enough, we can only respond, "Please don't judge me until you've walked a mile in my shoes."

Do I let others judge me or do I acknowledge my own growth today?

THOUGHT FOR THE DAY

I deserve to feel good about my accomplishments.

Life—an Adventure

Every day can be an adventure. We can make a new friend, learn something new about ourselves, or go somewhere new. The possibilities are endless.

Life is an adventure, one that offers us the known and the unknown, triumphs and adversities, joys and sorrows, and possibilities never considered. Rather than fear it or try to hide from it, let us embrace it.

Do I embrace my life today?

Thought for the Day

I can live life each day as the adventure it is.

MAY

• MAY 1 •

WEEKLY MEETINGS

The people in a weekly support group can become our family, a guide on our journey. They can be our pillars of strength and, ultimately, our conscience. They can offer love and care when we cannot care for and love ourselves.

In spite of our illness, these are people in our peer support meetings who will remain loyal and trusting. They won't care what medication we're on or if we've been hospitalized. They will fully support us whatever we're going through. They can help us to laugh again and be there for us when we need to cry. Through *their* acceptance, we can come to better accept our illness and ourselves.

Do I have a support group to help me on my journey today? If not, will I seek one out?

THOUGHT FOR THE DAY

*I need a place where I am supported
and loved unconditionally, a place where I belong.*

· M A Y 2 ·

A COMMITMENT TO RECOVERY

What is my commitment to my recovery today? Do
I take my medications? Do I see my doctor if I need
to? Do I carry out my physical, mental, and spiritual
exercises and practices regularly?

Recovery needs to be the highest priority in our
life. Our life depends on it. We cannot afford to become lax. Each day when we awaken, we must make
a commitment to ourselves, our Higher Power, and
others who care about us that recovery is our top
priority.

Today, do I make a fresh and full commitment to my
recovery?

THOUGHT FOR THE DAY

Daily commitment is my key to recovery.

Not Just Black and White

For many of us with a mental illness, there was a time when our lives were simply black (the hope-lessness that often consumed us) and white (the fake hope of the ideal self we were *supposed* to be).

But today there are new colors in our lives. We have found a positive attitude and effective ways of coping.

Hopelessness and unrealistic expectations may return from time to time, but through our process of healing, we now know that our world is not just black and white, but full of colors.

Do I see all the colors within and around me today?

Thought for the Day

*There is much more to life—and me—
than black and white.*

MATURITY AND MENTAL ILLNESS

When we first begin managing our illness, we are usually learning to live our lives anew—at times a complicated and difficult process. We lack maturity.

Gradually we learn to cope with and manage our illness. Little by little, we learn about ourselves and our illness. We fall but rise to our feet again. We learn what made us fall and what gave us the courage to get up.

This is the way we gain strength, wisdom, and maturity. We come to know our illness, our souls, ourselves.

Am I learning to manage and cope with my illness a bit more today and every day?

THOUGHT FOR THE DAY

Maturity is a process of coming to know myself and my illness better and better.

TAKING RISKS

Fear can be overwhelming, even paralyzing. It can keep us from leaving our homes. We may even get to the point where we feel there are no safe sidewalks to walk, no safe places to visit.

Overcoming and coping with fear takes courage and the willingness to take risks. Taking these risks, however, will eventually lead to a sense of freedom and safety.

We can begin by taking our first risk—the one in front of us—right now. Then, one step at a time, we find ourselves feeling safe, free, and at home in the world.

Have I taken my first step toward freedom and safety today by taking a reasonable risk?

THOUGHT FOR THE DAY

Sometimes, in order to feel safe
I must first feel temporarily unsafe.

• MAY 6 •

TRUSTING

There are bound to be times when we become impatient and lose faith. Instead of trusting in our Higher Power and letting matters unfold, we take them into our own hands. As the saying goes, we push the river instead of letting it flow by itself.

But pushing a river is a lot of work. Rather than staying on our natural course and schedule, we're more likely to run aground.

Can I let go today and trust in my Higher Power?

THOUGHT FOR THE DAY

Faith is the antidote for the need to be in control.

CELEBRATION DAY

We do not need complete freedom from our illness to live a full life. We need only do our best to accept our condition and its limitations.

When we reach this point of understanding, it is a day worth celebrating. It is a day in which we are no longer a prisoner of our illness, when we begin to feel gratitude for what we have in our lives. We have hope and we trust ourselves and our future. We begin to love ourselves just as we are.

Is today a day of celebration for me?

THOUGHT FOR THE DAY

Accepting myself as I am
is an essential step toward healing.

OPTIONS

In the early stages of learning to manage our illness, when we tried to do something we used to be able to do, the result was often *I can't. I can't* became a way of protecting ourselves.

But as we learn more about managing our illness, we come to understand just what our limitations really are. Our attitude then shifts from *I can't* to *Let me try and see* and *I tried and wasn't able to, so I'll try another way.* With this attitude come options, optimism, and eventual success.

Today, do I look for options and new ways of making things work?

THOUGHT FOR THE DAY

*When something isn't possible, I can let go of it.
And when something is possible, let me give it a try.*

A Chance at Serenity and Peace

We were up, then down, then up again. We were angry and arrogant; we were gregarious and beneficent. We had money; we were broke. We were sober one day and drunk the next. We were free one day, in chains the next. Did we behave ourselves? How could we? We were mentally ill.

But one day, we learned about a treatment plan for our mental illness. We were told it would not cure us, but it would help us stay focused long enough to learn what we needed to do to develop some stability in our lives. Soon we began getting help.

Today we still have a mental illness. There is no cure as yet. But with the treatments available to us, we have a chance at a life of serenity and peace. And for that we can be grateful.

Today, do I remind myself that appropriate treatment can help me find peace and serenity?

Thought for the Day

Stability leads to serenity.

BELIEVING IN MIRACLES

Many of us have come to believe in miracles for one reason: we are alive today through the grace of our Higher Power—working through caring people and through our revitalized spirit.

Miracles take place every day. Some we see; some we are don't. Some are vivid and profound; others are quiet and subtle. Some happen to others and some happen to us.

Today, do I realize the wonder of my life?

THOUGHT FOR THE DAY

Life is a miracle; I am a miracle.

THE ROAD OF RECOVERY

Recovery is a personal process that starts with accepting our illness and continues with changing our attitudes, values, and goals.

On our road of recovery, we can come to know and appreciate ourselves as never before. We can come to celebrate our strengths and humbly accept our limitations. We can learn the meaning of perseverance and become grateful for who we are becoming.

Have I traveled farther down the road of recovery today?

THOUGHT FOR THE DAY

I have my own road of recovery.

Learning to Love Ourselves

Those of us with a mental illness know what it feels like to hate ourselves. For many of us, this hate came about as we discovered our illness. Though we must live with the illness, we do not have to live with self-hate and shame.

We can turn our hatred into love by accepting who we are and forgiving ourselves for past behavior. If we can do this, our hatred and shame will begin to fade, and love and self-acceptance will begin to fill our souls.

Today, no matter how I may feel about my mental illness, can I love myself exactly as I am?

Thought for the Day

*Acceptance and forgiveness are the beginnings
of genuine love.*

HEALING TOUCH

There's a healing touch waiting for each of us. It comes from our Higher Power. It can cure our sadness. It can save us in times of inner turmoil and self-doubt. When we allow our Higher Power into our life, this healing touch will find us.

Do I let my Higher Power into my life today?

THOUGHT FOR THE DAY

My Higher Power's healing touch is waiting for me.
All I need to do is ask for it.

AVOIDING SELF-DEFEATING BEHAVIORS

Self-defeating behaviors can harm us emotionally, physically, and spiritually. But if we recognize them for what they are and cope with the short-term pain, we will get more relief in the long-term.

We learned our self-defeating behaviors over time; they may have become our first response to any uncomfortable feeling or situation. But just as we learned them, we can also unlearn them. As we begin to recognize them, we can begin confronting them, and eventually avoid them completely.

Today, do I use new self-affirming behaviors to cope with my uncomfortable feelings and situations?

THOUGHT FOR THE DAY

Self-defeating behaviors can be unlearned.

THE REALITY OF OUR ILLNESS

Most of us have fantasized about our illness simply disappearing, and about living lives free of pain and hardship. It is very appealing, especially when our illness is active and we are in turmoil and severe emotional pain.

Fantasizing is normal. But we must be cautious when entertaining our fantasies, or fantasy and reality may become indistinguishable. We may begin to think, believe, and act as if we do not have an illness—and then stop managing our illness and our life.

Today, are my fantasies healthy, or do I let them become my reality?

THOUGHT FOR THE DAY

The good that comes from taking care of myself is better than any fantasy.

• MAY 16 •

PRACTICING PATIENCE

Our illness may have paralyzed some of us for a time. We may now feel the need to go ahead at "full steam" and do everything we missed out on.

But by moving too fast and trying to redeem the past, we can easily lose perspective. It is easier to maintain perspective if we can practice patience.

Do I practice patience today?

THOUGHT FOR THE DAY

If I put my emotional, physical, and spiritual health first, and practice patience, the rest will follow.

WILL TO LIVE

With mental illness, one minute we may have the desire to die and the next minute we have the will to live. One minute can be filled with hope and the next with despair. Our emotions change with the wind. It isn't that we want it this way. It's just the nature of our illness.

For most of us, the desire to live is far greater than the desire to die. But when our illness becomes intensely active, the desire to die is sometimes all we can think about. But if we realize how this cycle works, we can change our thinking and begin confronting our thoughts. We learn that we can cope with them, instead of acting on them.

Our illness may sometimes give us despair and thoughts of self-harm, but as we grow stronger and wiser, we learn that our will to live is much stronger.

Today, is my will to live stronger than my desire to die? If not, do I seek help?

THOUGHT FOR THE DAY

*Despair and the urge to die will pass
when I seek the help of others.*

Unexpected Symptoms

We can be going about our lives for weeks, months, or even years without incident. Then suddenly our illness calls. Some of us may adjust to the symptoms; others may find their lives drastically altered.

Some of us have learned how to predict our cycles, while for others who are still learning, the cycles may remain unpredictable. What is most important, however, is that we learn from our past experience, react wisely, and seek help from others when our illness calls.

Today, do I know how to react, cope, and ask for help if my illness comes calling?

Thought for the Day

How I have coped in the past can become my guide when the present is unpredictable.

• MAY 19 •

A NEW LIFE

Because of our illness, we are learning how to live a new life. A life with new rules, boundaries, and limitations—but new possibilities as well. A life that holds more hope and promise than disappointment and despair. A life dedicated to healing.

Today, do I believe that I can live a new life in spite of my illness?

THOUGHT FOR THE DAY

Mental illness can become an opportunity to learn about myself and grow spiritually.

SOURCES OF HELP

Many of us with a mental illness think we are alone when it comes to managing our illness. But we're not. Many resources are available to us: professionals, national organizations, local support groups, and other people who have a mental illness. All we have to do is ask.

Do I know what resources are available to me today and where to find them?

THOUGHT FOR THE DAY

Managing my illness means reaching out for help when I need it.

• MAY 21 •

When Nothing Mattered

There was a time for most of us when nothing mattered anymore. The beginning of a new day was just a continuation of the pain and hopelessness of yesterday and the day before that. We had no dreams, for our illness had taken them away. Shame and self-hatred were consuming. We decided we were unlovable—physically and emotionally defective. Some of us tried taking our own lives.

Now things can change. We can regain real hope and faith in ourselves. We can have dreams and work to fulfill them. We can come to love ourselves and accept our illness. We no longer need look at our lives as if nothing really matters. We are on the road of recovery.

Today, do I recognize just how far I have come in my recovery?

Thought for the Day

The fact that I've traveled this far on my journey of recovery is a cause for gratitude.

• MAY 22 •

PROCESS OR RESULT?

When we begin managing our illness, most of us do it with earnest effort and the best of intentions. But we can't do it perfectly. We need to experiment with techniques and approaches. Some will work for us; others will not.

But when something doesn't work, we have not failed. We simply ask ourselves whether we have put forth our best effort and can learn from our mistakes. When it comes to managing our illness, the only way to fail is not to try.

Today, do I punish myself for failure or do I learn from my mistakes?

THOUGHT FOR THE DAY

*Trial and error give me the freedom
to learn what will work for me.*

CONSUMED BY ILLNESS

There have been times when our illness was all we could think about. We wanted to sleep, we tried to work, but our illness never left our side. We were obsessed. We couldn't help ourselves nor pursue other interests because the illness guided every thought and action. It became the center of our universe.

But today, we are grateful to have found some balance. The illness remains part of our lives, but we have learned to live with it and manage it. It is still our companion, but it no longer need be an obsession.

Today, do I remember that I am bigger than my illness and that it is only a part of who I am?

THOUGHT FOR THE DAY

I am more than my illness.

THE FOUNDATION OF OUR LIFE

Each moment we contribute to the foundation of our life. Our Higher Power has a plan for us for today, tomorrow, and the journey ahead. All things will be revealed when we're ready and seek the needed guidance.

We need only trust the process and be willing to do whatever work is necessary to continue our journey.

Today, do I let my Higher Power add a new layer to the foundation of my life?

THOUGHT FOR THE DAY

There is a plan for me.

· MAY 25 ·

WE HAVE COME A LONG WAY

When we look back at our first days, weeks, and months of recovery, we can see that we have come a long way. We went from a state of hopelessness to a life of hope. From imprisonment by our illness to freedom of mind, body, and spirit. From a place devoid of dreams to a place where dreams are not only imaginable but attainable. From a place of self-hatred to a place of self-acceptance and love.

Let us acknowledge the work we have accomplished and express gratitude for the gifts we have been given.

Today, do I realize and appreciate how much I have accomplished with the guidance of my Higher Power?

THOUGHT FOR THE DAY

Step by step, one day at a time,
I have what it takes to continue my journey.

• MAY 26 •

TAKING A BREAK

As our recovery progresses, so do our responsibilities and commitments. Before we know it, weeks and months have passed with no time for ourselves. When we do this, we put ourselves in danger—emotionally, physically, and spiritually.

There comes a time when we need to say to ourselves, *I need a break. I deserve a break. I'm going to take a break.* Then we must make sure we take it. We cannot afford to get run down. We need to take care of ourselves.

If needed, do I take a break today?

THOUGHT FOR THE DAY

Taking a break when I need it
means I value and protect my health.

Rebuilding and Maintaining Our Social Lives

For many of us with a mental illness, life revolved around ourselves and our illness, at least for a time. Many of us could not reach out to our families, friends, or people in the community to do the things we liked to do. Some of us could not leave home. Our social lives faded away and we fell into isolation.

But today we know that we can no longer afford to live in loneliness and isolation. We need to take a risk and reach out to others. We need to begin rebuilding and maintaining our social lives.

For some of us, this is still a frightening prospect. Yet only when we break free from our isolation can we rebuild our social life (and even discover new friendships and new freedom).

Today, do I reach out to others and begin building bonds?

Thought for the Day

Reaching out and connecting with others is an essential part of my recovery.

Being Consistent

To manage our illness, we must be consistent with what keeps us healthy—emotionally, physically, and spiritually. We cannot afford to take our medications or get adequate sleep or attend support groups just when it's convenient.

Yet learning to be consistent takes time, practice, and patience. If we practice every day, one day at a time, we will soon become consistent.

Am I consistent in managing my illness today?

Thought for the Day

*Consistency means taking care of myself
each and every day.*

DUAL DISORDERS

Many of us with a mental illness are also dependent on alcohol or other drugs. We have two illnesses that demand our attention. We tend to use alcohol or other drugs (or both) to relieve our symptoms. But eventually they only make our lives worse.

Yet recovery from dual disorders is possible. Each day we remain clean and sober we gain strength, courage, and the wisdom to cope.

Today, am I committed to my dual disorders recovery?

THOUGHT FOR THE DAY

*Having dual disorders requires
having a dual recovery program.*

LETTING GO OF SHAME

The arrival of a mental illness can leave us morally and spiritually distressed. The solid relationship we have had with our Higher Power can seem to vanish. We may feel ashamed because of our illness and what it made us do, and feel unworthy of such a bond.

But as we begin to heal, the shame will diminish. More and more we will come to accept ourselves and forgive ourselves. Slowly, we envision a renewed and stronger relationship with our Higher Power.

Today, do I practice letting go of shame?

THOUGHT FOR THE DAY

My Higher Power remains with me even when my shame makes me feel unworthy.

PACING

Sometimes we can't help but get excited about plans we've made. But then we discover that our energy has run out and we wonder what's wrong.

What happened was that we forgot to pace ourselves. Although our mind thought otherwise, our body did not have time to restore itself.

In our new way of life, it's important to set a pace that is realistic. Everything will get done. Everything will unfold in its own time. Tomorrow will arrive when the sun comes up, and not before.

Am I pacing myself on my journey today?

THOUGHT FOR THE DAY

Life is not a race.

JUNE

• J U N E   1 •

A Chronic Illness

Like any illness, we neither expected nor wanted to have a mental health disorder. But like with other illnesses, no one has a choice about who and when mental illness strikes.

Over time, we are getting to know it better; the pain, loneliness, and uncertainty it brings—as well as the stigma. Yet over time, it's getting easier to accept it for what it is: a no-fault, chronic illness. And just because an illness is chronic, does not mean it has to define us.

Today, do I accept my illness a little more?

Thought for the Day

The more I know about my illness, the easier it is to accept it, learn from it, and recover from it.

• J U N E   2 •

THE VALUE OF FRIENDS

When we meet with friends, our hearts are warmed. Good friends can be loving, caring, and nonjudgmental. They share their feelings, insights, strengths, and hopes with us. They help us laugh. They comfort us when we cry. They are with us in times of need and refuse to leave us in times of crisis. In bad times they make our lives more bearable; in good times they add to our joy.

Am I grateful for my friendships today?

THOUGHT FOR THE DAY

Every friendship is a huge gift—to both parties.

COMING TO TERMS WITH FEAR

Fear has struck each and every one of us with mental illness. It has touched all areas of our lives. We feared our illness, our past, our present, and our future. We may have even feared our family and friends. Some of us were afraid of ourselves.

Fear is natural. But it becomes unhealthy when we let it run our lives and make all of our decisions.

Coming to terms with our fear requires that we look beyond the fear itself. Usually there is a secondary reason for fear behind what we think is causing it. When we discover what that is and face it, we no longer have to let fear control our every action. We can make choices that are not based on our fears.

Do I work on coming to terms with my fears today?

THOUGHT FOR THE DAY

When I come to terms with my fears, I find freedom.

• J U N E   4 •

PARENTS WITH MENTAL ILLNESS

Many of us who cope with mental illness are parents or have responsibility for other people in our lives. When we're well, we try every day to be first-rate parents or caretakers. But some days, our illness takes over and we can't give our all. Then we just do the best we can and pray for their understanding.

Let us make the most of the good days and avoid getting lost in regret or guilt.

Today, do I make the most of my time with the people I care for?

THOUGHT FOR THE DAY

*I am a caring person with a chronic illness
that is not my fault.*

• JUNE 5 •

OUR RELATIONSHIP WITH OUR HIGHER POWER

We don't have to impress our Higher Power. We can simply trust that there is a Power greater than ourselves that does not require anything special from us, that accepts us as we are.

We can think of our Higher Power as a friend who is always ready to listen. Our Higher Power will give us what is best for us, though it may not be what we expect or desire.

We can share all of our secrets and our shortcomings and not be ashamed.

No matter how we may feel, or what we may believe, or how angry we become, this Power will be there for us.

Do I trust that my Higher Power is there for me today?

THOUGHT FOR THE DAY

*Even when my faith fades or all seems hopeless,
I am not alone.*

✳

FINDING HUMOR IN OUR ILLNESS

From time to time, our illness can put us in some compromising and embarrassing situations. Learning to laugh at them can be one of our greatest assets in coping.

Laughing may not come easily. False pride, perfectionism, and a need to rise above every situation may get in the way.

Yet we all have a sense of humor and it can shine through the barriers we have built. We can find humor where there was once embarrassment and anguish.

Am I stuck in pride and perfectionism today or can I find the humor in my illness?

THOUGHT FOR THE DAY

When I can laugh at myself, I can better love myself.

• J U N E 7 •

No Use Complaining

Our world, and the people who share it with us, are far from perfect. So if we choose, we can find plenty to complain about. But what's the use? What do we gain? Who really listens, anyway? Besides, by merely complaining, we rarely get what we want or solve the problem. In fact, we often make the situation worse.

On the other hand, we can choose to see our disappointments and problems as challenges—and sometimes as opportunities—rather than as reasons to complain.

Do I complain about everything today or do I look for opportunities and solutions?

Thought for the Day

When I focus on complaints, I can't see solutions; when I focus on opportunities, solutions and choices emerge.

WHEN OTHERS DON'T UNDERSTAND

There are many myths and misconceptions about mental illness. Not everyone has a full understanding of what these illnesses are, or of the symptoms they produce.

So when others do not understand, or are quick to judge our behavior or our illness, let us not react out of frustration or a feeling of inadequacy. Let us not hold them in contempt. Instead, let us recognize that many people have yet to learn about mental illness and many are afraid and not yet ready to learn.

Let us teach those who are willing to listen and be patient with those who are not. If we do, we will learn about ourselves as well.

Do I have patience and tolerance for others—and myself—today?

THOUGHT FOR THE DAY

Teaching takes place only when
others are willing to learn.

❋

BEING HONEST WITH OURSELVES

Some of us have a difficult time being honest with ourselves about our illness—and even about our life. We may tell ourselves that the pain we endured or the things we did weren't as serious as they actually were. Or we tell ourselves that our lives have not really changed because of our illness, or that our illness has had little or no effect on anyone around us.

But when we're honest with ourselves, we are sure to discover that, for the most part, this just isn't so.

Being honest with ourselves about our illness and our life is difficult, but it can be done. It begins when we look at ourselves and our situation as they truly are, not as we want them to be or think they should be.

Am I honest with myself today?

THOUGHT FOR THE DAY

Nothing nurtures recovery more than simple honesty.

• JUNE 10 •

WHERE OUR GIFTS COME FROM

The gift of recovery, and all that it offers, comes not only from our own efforts, but also from other people and our Higher Power.

Perhaps we have crossed oceans and climbed mountains to arrive at this point in our recovery. We can be proud of how far we have come and all the work we have done.

But let us not forget the support and strength we have received from a Power greater than ourselves—which includes other people. Let us realize that what has taken place is nothing short of a miracle.

Today, do I remind myself that my recovery is a gift from my Higher Power?

THOUGHT FOR THE DAY

Recovery means not having to do everything myself.

• JUNE 11 •

HOW I FEEL TODAY

Am I angry, anxious, apathetic, or bored? Confident, confused, or curious? Determined, disappointed, enthusiastic, envious, or excited? Peaceful, proud, or puzzled? Regretful, relieved, or satisfied?

As we go through our day, it is imperative that we know just how we are feeling, so that we can manage, cope with, and learn from our emotions. If we do not know how we're feeling, we may respond inappropriately, hurt ourselves, or hurt someone else.

As we identify our feelings, we can write them down or share them with others—whichever way makes it easier for us to name them.

Do I stay in touch with my feelings today?

THOUGHT FOR THE DAY

If I know how I feel, I can cope with my emotions.

• J U N E   1 2 •

A Place Where We Belong

Many of us have been searching for a place where we belong, a place where we can be ourselves, where we no longer have to hide the fact of our illness.

Though it is elusive at times, this place is neither imaginary nor external: it lies within us. Too often we only look to the world around us for acceptance and comfort when in fact they can be available within ourselves.

Today, do I look within for comfort and acceptance?

Thought for the Day

The acceptance and comfort I seek lies within me.

SURRENDERING TO REALITY

Some of us are still not sure that we have a mental illness. For some of us, this fight is continuous and painful. Even worse, our denial only leads us further and further away from recovery.

If we are to be at peace with our illness and ourselves, we must admit that our illness is at times much greater than we are. If we are to be at peace with our illness and find serenity, we must turn to a Power greater than ourselves.

Do I surrender to the truth about my illness today?

THOUGHT FOR THE DAY

*Simply by surrendering to the fact that I have
a mental illness and cannot get well again on my own, I
am already on the road to peace and recovery.*

RELATIONSHIPS

Many of us with a mental illness have struggled with relationships. We may not accept ourselves and our illness and therefore think others will not accept us because we have an illness. When we think this way, we are likely to isolate ourselves from other people.

But if we want to build relationships and allow intimacy in our lives, we must begin to take risks. This may be difficult and fearful in the beginning. But the more we accept ourselves and the more we reach out, the easier it gets.

Am I willing to take the first step in building a relationship today?

THOUGHT FOR THE DAY

I can begin to form relationships
by accepting myself and reaching out.

• J U N E   1 5 •

HOLDING ON

Most of us have days when we feel like we just can't go on anymore. We can't take the stress and the emotions. We just want relief. Sometimes this is a normal response to everyday life, other times it's due to our illness.

Either way, when these days arrive, we need to reach out to family, friends, professionals, or anyone else in our support network who can provide relief. When we reach out for help, we are taking a step toward serenity and recovery. And soon we realize that we can make it after all.

If I feel I just can't go on anymore today, do I reach out and ask for help?

THOUGHT FOR THE DAY

*I have to live through just one situation
and one day at a time.*

OUR SPIRITUAL JOURNEY

We begin our spiritual journey at different times in our lives but most of us reach the same place eventually, where we accept the guidance of a Power greater than ourselves. A Power that cares for us and accepts us just as we are. A Power that guides us, teaches us, and grants us just what we need— and, at times, what we want. A Power that helps us cope with our illness each day. A Power that never leaves our side, even when we become angry and demanding.

If we have not yet begun our spiritual journey, there is still time to do so. Our Higher Power is there for us. All that is required from us is the willingness to begin.

Today, have I begun my spiritual journey?

THOUGHT FOR THE DAY

Spirituality is a gift that is always available.

• J U N E 1 7 •

RECLAIMING OUR LIVES

Reclaiming our lives does not mean total freedom from our illness and its symptoms, nor from our difficulties. But it can mean freedom from the worst we've experienced.

We no longer need to be a prisoner of our illness. We can know peace where there was once despair, and find faith where there was once hopelessness.

The first steps are accepting ourselves and our illness, reaching out to others who can help, and turning to our Higher Power for guidance.

Am I reclaiming my life today?

THOUGHT FOR THE DAY

Reclaiming my life is a choice; it means accepting who I am while being willing to change.

OUR HIGHER POWER LOVES US

In times of confusion and emotional turmoil, some of us have railed at our Higher Power. We were angry about all that had happened to us, full of resentment, and in need of someone to blame. Some of us even tried forcing our Higher Power out of our lives.

And yet, no matter what we said, our Higher Power never left us. It was usually *we* who left when we did not get what we demanded. Let us never forget that our Higher Power loves us and cares for us, regardless of what we do.

Do I know that my Higher Power is unconditionally accepting of me today?

THOUGHT FOR THE DAY

In turmoil or good health,
my Higher Power is always by my side.

ALL WHO HAVE CARED

What would we have done if not for the people who cared for us over the years? They may not have known about our illness at first, but as time passed and our trust grew, they were eager to learn. They stepped in at the right time, understood us, and accepted us.

They often cared for us when we could not care for ourselves. They helped us get back on our feet and watched us climb up from the depths of despair. Because of them we could find peace and a way to cope with our illness. For all of this we can be grateful.

Is there someone in my life who helped me when I could not help myself? Am I grateful to that person today?

THOUGHT FOR THE DAY

Accepting the help of others teaches humility—
a spiritual quality necessary for quality recovery.

❀

• JUNE 20 •

SELF-PITY OR GRATITUDE?

When our circumstances are painful or difficult, it's normal to feel some self-pity. But when we allow self-pity to fester, it can make our illness worse. Without realizing it, our attitude can turn from hope and faith to hopelessness and despair.

But what self-pity has created we can also uncreate, if we so desire. We can start focusing on feeling gratitude for all of the good things in our life (and for life itself).

Today, do I let self-pity consume me or do I focus on gratitude?

THOUGHT FOR THE DAY

When times are hard, a little self-pity can be healthy, while just a little more can be destructive.

THE LINK IN THE CHAIN

In spite of our desires and best intentions, our illness can appear from nowhere and tempt us to do something that harms us or others.

To maintain our recovery, we must learn to recognize when we are vulnerable. We must learn to recognize and manage the harmful messages our illness sends us. Let us begin to strengthen this link in the chain, so that this too is a day of recovery for us.

Am I monitoring myself carefully today, and doing all I can to maintain my recovery?

THOUGHT FOR THE DAY

Recovery takes place one minute at a time, one hour at a time, and one day at a time.

· JUNE 22 ·

LEARNING TO LIVE WITH A MENTAL ILLNESS

Learning to live with a mental illness is a process. We are always growing, learning, accepting and re-accepting. At every step, the process includes emotional and spiritual growth. Although it may bring us to our knees, it teaches us humility and perseverance, and it helps us to rise to our feet once again.

But most of all, learning to live with a mental illness is about learning to live with ourselves.

Am I learning to live with myself and my illness today?

THOUGHT FOR THE DAY

Learning to live with myself and my illness
is sometimes humbling and sometimes painful,
but always valuable.

LOVING OURSELVES FIRST

At some point, many of us with mental illness concluded that we were unworthy of being loved. We assumed that because we were different, we didn't deserve love. We searched everywhere, hoping to find someone who would care for us.

But eventually we discovered that we had been searching in the wrong places. We sought the love and approval of others before we had come to love and approve of ourselves.

Needing the love and approval of others is natural, but part of recovery is also learning to love ourselves. For when we love ourselves, we are better able to accept and appreciate the love of others.

Am I learning to love myself today?

THOUGHT FOR THE DAY

*Wanting others to love me is not unhealthy,
but loving myself is essential to my recovery.*

✸

Not Me!

Chances are, we never thought we would experience a mental illness; never thought we would become isolated or at times lose all hope; never thought suicide might become an obsession; never thought we could be institutionalized; never thought we could act so out of control, often against our morals or values.

We also probably never thought we could find hope and recover; never thought we could learn to cope with the illness, be reasonably content with ourselves, and live each day as best we can. Yet all of this can happen to us.

Today, am I stuck in what I think should happen or fear might happen—or am I focused on what is possible here and now?

Thought for the Day

Although life is full of unknowns and surprises,
I can make the choice each moment to affirm my life.

❋

• J U N E   2 5 •

No Guarantees

We don't know when our next worsening of symptoms will occur, how long it will last, how long it will take to recover. We don't know how long our medications will remain effective nor whether a cure will be found for our illness. We can't know the future nor fully control the present.

But we can learn to do the best with what we are given, accept the rest, and cope with the unpredictable. Today we have one day in which to live and do our best.

Today, do I search for guarantees or do I live my life one day at a time?

Thought for the Day

Why spend my time looking for guarantees when I can live life to the fullest this very moment?

Hanging On

There are days when we wonder why we should even get out of bed. Our symptoms are severe. Our serenity has disappeared. Our attitude is grim. We are at odds with ourselves.

On these days, it is enough to just hang on. We don't have to feel guilty or pretend to be healthy or worry about our to-do list. Instead, we simply call a friend or someone in our support system and let that person know how we're doing.

If today is a day when all I can do is hang on, can I acknowledge that fact, let go of my plans, and reach out for help?

Thought for the Day

I can't control when my symptoms flare,
but I can take care of myself when they do

· JUNE 27 ·

LEARNING AND SHARING

Let us take a moment to congratulate ourselves. We have graduated from the School of Hard Knocks into a life of recovery.

We have paid steep tuition: our illness and its symptoms. But we learned a lot and we did not give up. Of this we can be proud.

Being in recovery means that we can now teach what we have learned. We can offer to share our experience and wisdom to those just beginning their journey.

Today, do I continue to learn and share my understanding?

THOUGHT FOR THE DAY

Recovery is a continuous cycle
of learning, teaching, listening, and sharing.

· JUNE 28 ·

GREAT EXPECTATIONS

It is normal to have expectations of ourselves and expectations for our future. But if they become too great, we can set ourselves up for failure.

We can either make our expectations impossible or keep them realistic. We can make them part of our illness or positive forces in our recovery. They can make us feel like a failure or a success. They can become an enemy or a helpful guide. The choice is ours.

Do I have healthy expectations today?

THOUGHT FOR THE DAY

If I fail to meet my expectations, I am gentle with myself because I am still learning to be realistic.

• J U N E 2 9 •

Seeking Professional Guidance

Some of us with depression or mental illness find it difficult, and sometimes impossible, to seek professional guidance for our illness. Yet professional guidance may be critical if we are to survive.

With an illness such as ours, self-reliance can be dangerous, even fatal. Mental illness is a medical condition that demands regular attention by professionals, just like asthma or diabetes. For the sake of our emotional and physical health, for the sake of our recovery, let us seek the professional guidance and support we need and deserve.

Will I seek professional guidance for my illness if I need it today?

Thought for the Day

There is no shame in asking for help.

CAREFUL MONITORING

Once we come to know our illness and learn to cope with it, we may decide one day to take recovery into our own hands. That's okay.

But if we begin to experience impatience, intolerance, or lose control of our thoughts and feelings, it may be time to seek help.

Today, do I continue to trust in my judgment as well as the judgment of other people and my Higher Power?

THOUGHT FOR THE DAY

I need to do whatever is necessary for my spiritual, emotional, and physical health.

JULY

• J U L Y   1 •

Holding Sacred and Being Held

At times, we all need someone to hold us. Sometimes we need someone to hold us and say nothing. At other times we need someone to tell us that everything will be okay. We need to feel safe and know that we are not alone. We need to know that someone else cares and will be here for us, both in triumph and despair.

But what we need most is for someone to hold us sacred. Someone to let us know that no matter what we have done or how awful we may feel, they believe in us and love us. They love us for who we are this very moment and not for who we may someday become.

Do I allow others to hold me sacred and give me what I need today?

Thought for the Day

Being held, whether physically or spiritually, contains a sacred healing power to be treasured.

FREEDOM OF OPPORTUNITY

If we think about it for a moment, finding recovery can be like winning the lottery. No, we didn't win millions of dollars. In recovery we win something more valuable: the chance for a new life.

We are no longer prisoners of our illness. Yes, we still have some limitations, but freedom of opportunity is ours.

Do I appreciate the opportunities I have today?

THOUGHT FOR THE DAY

Illness limits my freedom; recovery reclaims it.

• J U L Y 3 •

But for the Grace of God

There but for the grace of God go I. How true this is for many of us. Our situation could have been far worse. We arrived at this point in our recovery through the grace of our Higher Power—the God of our understanding.

Let us embrace and be grateful for the many gifts our Higher Power has given us. Let us share them graciously with others.

Do I realize where my gifts come from today?

Thought for the Day

When I am grateful for and share the gifts
I have been given, I am more likely to keep them.

• J U L Y 4 •

INDEPENDENCE DAY

Independence is relative. For those of us with a mental illness, it means living our lives as best we can in spite of our illness.

Many of us can recall when we were entirely at the mercy of our illness. But in each moment, step by step, we are reclaiming our lives and our independence.

Do I value the independence I have in my life today?

THOUGHT FOR THE DAY

Independence is measured individually and achieved one moment at a time.

NEGATIVE TALK AND HEALING TALK

If we tell ourselves we are worthless because of our illness, we may never be able to appreciate our successes. If we tell ourselves no one will love us because of our illness, then we may not allow others to love us. If we tell ourselves our lives are over, then we may not take advantage of all our opportunities.

We have no room left for healing talk if we bombard ourselves with negative thoughts.

To begin to heal ourselves emotionally we can give ourselves positive messages and accept compliments from others. When we do this consistently, we steadily create a positive self-image.

What do I tell myself about myself today?

THOUGHT FOR THE DAY

Healing messages promote healing actions.

• J U L Y 6 •

ONE DAY AT A TIME

Some of us took a long time to seek help, to choose recovery. We were self-destructive. Some of us abused alcohol or other drugs, and further undermined our stability. People suffered because of our actions. We were desperate and hopeless.

But one day, we managed to reach out. Slowly we picked ourselves up from the bottom. With help, we stopped using alcohol and street drugs, and we started getting treatment for our mental illness. It has been a long journey, but we have survived and we are getting healthier all the time.

Today, do I realize how far I have come on my journey?

THOUGHT FOR THE DAY

No matter where I began my journey,
I am capable of recovery.

• J U L Y 7 •

Walking by Faith as well as by Sight

Faith is not visible. It comes from within. It can guide us both in triumph and despair. It can make the impossible possible. It can resonate throughout the universe.

On our journey, many paths we go down will require our faith rather than our sight. Walking by faith requires us to believe that something greater than ourselves is with us and guides us at all times.

Do I walk only by sight alone today or is faith my companion?

Thought for the Day

No matter how well I may see with my eyes,
I can still be blind without faith.

A Higher Power on Our Spiritual Journey

None of us on a spiritual journey has the same spiritual path. But early on in the journey we all share a process of accepting into our lives a Power greater than ourselves. A Power that accepts us as we are. A Power that can teach us and give us what we need. A Power that can provide the strength and comfort to help us cope with our illness.

Our Higher Power is always available to us. All we need is the desire and the willingness to begin the journey.

Today, do I acknowledge a Higher Power on my spiritual journey?

Thought for the Day

Recovery is a spiritual journey.

SETTING OUR OWN PACE

Many of us with a mental illness develop our own pace, based on the needs of our recovery. We're not too fast and we're not too slow.

Others may be faster, but we don't have to keep up with them. We stick to our own pace and do the best we can.

Do I stick to my own pace today?

THOUGHT FOR THE DAY

Recovery isn't a race, it's a process.

LETTING GO OF WORRY

Many of us with mental illness wonder when our next episode or cycle will occur. In doing so, we may forget to live our lives in the here and now.

Most of us will have another bout of our symptoms worsening one day. But until then, why should we spend time worrying? Rather than live from cycle to cycle, let us live one day at a time. Let us set up a plan for dealing with episodes when they occur. Then we can live fully in each moment. Then we can let ourselves feel good when we feel good.

Do I live in the worries of tomorrow or do I embrace the joys and challenges of today?

THOUGHT FOR THE DAY

When I appreciate what is taking place right now,
I forget to worry.

BECOMING

As we progress on our journey, we will discover and rediscover our deepest beliefs, our values, who we are and who we have been teaching ourselves to become. It is an important, extended process.

If we approach our life as a process, we offer ourselves a new beginning every day. Each day we get to learn about ourselves and to practice what we have learned.

Today, do I know and live by my values?

THOUGHT FOR THE DAY

The process of discovery and recovery
teaches me who I am.

• J U L Y   1 2 •

SELF-EMPOWERMENT

Self-empowerment does not mean controlling others or having grandiose beliefs about ourselves. Rather, it means nurturing our inner strength and continually creating healthy situations for ourselves. It means accepting our assets as well as our defects. It means being aware of our self-defeating behaviors, coping with them, and when we can, replacing them with self-affirming ones. For many of us, it simply means learning about our illness and how to recover.

Do I seek self-empowerment today?

THOUGHT FOR THE DAY

Self-empowerment begins with honesty and humility.

DOING OUR PART

The chances of learning to cope with and effectively treating mental illness have greatly increased in recent years. Much knowledge has been gained. Medications have improved greatly and continue to improve.

But one aspect of recovery from a mental illness has not changed and never will: We must take responsibility for ourselves and for managing our illness.

Do I take responsibility for my own recovery today?

THOUGHT FOR THE DAY

*The miracle of recovery is due
to more than the wonders of modern medicine—
it is also due to the wonders of my strength and abilities.*

· J U L Y   1 4 ·

OTHERS LIKE US

There are others who, just like us, are living with a mental illness. They may live next door, down the street, or in the next neighborhood. Chances are, we have walked similar paths.

Perhaps they wonder if they are alone in this world with their illness; if there are others who might understand how they feel; if there are others who can share their own experience and offer a listening ear.

Perhaps they are waiting for someone like us to share with them our experience, strength, and hope.

When we feel alone and wonder if there are others like us, let us reach out. We will find that others will be there for us if we are there for them.

Have I reached out today and connected with others like me?

THOUGHT FOR THE DAY

When I reach out, I will inevitably find others like me.

TAKING CARE OF THE LITTLE THINGS

When the little problems begin to add up, it often leads to trouble. When we put off our daily affairs for any length of time, our lives can quickly become unmanageable. Like a snowball rolling down a hill—suddenly, we are crushed.

To avoid this, we must begin by attending to the small events in our lives. We must take care of them one by one. If they seem overwhelming, we can remind ourselves that we don't have to do them all at once, just one at a time.

Do I take care of the little things in my life today?

THOUGHT FOR THE DAY

Taking care of the little things prevents larger problems.

LIFE FROM A DISTANCE

Many of us have spent days, weeks, or months watching our life from a distance. We watched others reach their goals and dreams, but for us, life remained beyond some invisible horizon.

Today, we can start moving back into life—one minute, one hour, one situation at a time. Slowly we can begin acting on our desires and goals. Steadily, we can cope with whatever life puts before us.

Though our illness may hold us back from time to time, when well, we move forward on our journey.

Today, have I started living my life again?

THOUGHT FOR THE DAY

To live my life, I must be courageous and present.

A Family Affair

We may feel as though we are the only one affected by our illness, but that is not the case. When we are in emotional pain and turmoil, others feel our pain. When we are confused and afraid, others are confused and afraid for us. When we isolate ourselves, others fear for our safety and well-being. Mental illness is a family affair.

Instead of running away out of fear or embarrassment, let us keep everyone informed and include them in our recovery. Let us make our recovery a family affair.

Today, do I share who and what I am with those who care about me?

Thought for the Day

When I share of myself, I gain strength.

OVERWORKED AND OUT OF TOUCH

It's not hard for us to get out of touch with ourselves, our spiritual lives, and the need to manage our illness. It happens when our job or career become the focus of our lives, when we become too attached to financial gain, when we tie our self-esteem to our work, or when we use work to avoid the realities of our illness.

Yet our survival depends on being in touch with our illness and its symptoms; it depends on being in touch with ourselves emotionally, physically, and spiritually.

Today, do I keep my health and recovery first?

THOUGHT FOR THE DAY

My first priority is to stay in touch with myself.

DISCOVERING OUR CALM SPIRIT

When our spirit is calm, we can experience serenity and harmony—at peace with ourselves and the world around us, at one with our Higher Power. The more realistic our expectations, the calmer our spirit and the more likely we will know peace.

Can I find the calm spirit that lies within me today?

THOUGHT FOR THE DAY

To discover my calm spirit, I reach within to find both my true abilities and my limitations and set my expectations accordingly.

LENDING A HAND

On our journey we will have many opportunities to help people we care about. But are we willing? At times our illness will prevent us from helping; at times we just won't feel like it. Maybe we've had a rough day or we're not feeling compassionate.

Yet helping at those times can benefit us a great deal: lending a hand brings us closer to those we help, makes us feel good about ourselves, and may improve our mood.

Today, do I help those around me as best I can, whether I feel like it or not?

THOUGHT FOR THE DAY

Regardless of my problems, lending a helping hand brings the satisfaction of having something to offer others.

LIVING IN THE PRESENT

One of the most difficult tasks is living in the present—this very moment—and experiencing whatever is happening in our lives.

Though difficult, we can learn how to do it. For example, we can close our eyes, take some deep breaths, and focus only on what is happening right now. Practice will make it easier.

Today, do I live in the present moment?

THOUGHT FOR THE DAY

Living in the present can make the simplest event a wonderful and exciting experience.

STAYING ON TRACK

When coping with mental illness, we are certain to have days when our memory isn't working as we would like it to. Our mental list of tasks evaporates, and we wonder where to go and what to do next.

We can seek refuge in a more structured plan for each day. A written list can help us remember just what we need to accomplish, and guide us through the day. We can check off one task at a time and see progress.

Today, do I use some kind of structured plan to bring order to my day?

THOUGHT FOR THE DAY

*The simplest accomplishments
can bring the greatest rewards.*

MEDICATION ADJUSTMENTS

The medications we take for our illness are far from perfect. On occasion, adjustments are needed. Because these medications take time to reach therapeutic levels—and because we can't know if this will take one week or four—we may feel frightened and unsure of ourselves for a while.

During this time, it helps to stay in close contact with our support system. It also helps if we can be gentle with ourselves. We need to allow time for the medications to take hold, and time for ourselves to adjust, both emotionally and physically.

If adjustments are being made to my medications today, am I gentle with myself and in close touch with those who can help me?

THOUGHT FOR THE DAY

Time and self-care will help me
when my medications are being adjusted.

✺

PROBLEMS WORK THEMSELVES OUT

It's not the end of the world to have problems, whether they are relationship- or work-related, or if their source is physical or emotional.

With time, patience, and faith, things often have a way of working themselves out. We may think things can't get any worse, or that they will never get better, or even that it's the end for us. But over time, situations often improve—especially if we believe they will and work to improve them.

Let us give difficult circumstances a little time to work themselves out . And let us do our best to stay positive and patient.

Today, do I remember that problems often work themselves out over time?

THOUGHT FOR THE DAY

Some days my problems may seem like the end of the world, but experience reminds me that they're not.

EXPRESSING OUR CREATIVITY

When we express the creativity within us, we can change our mood and the way we feel about ourselves. Expressing creativity has the power to help us relax or become invigorated. It helps us grow, mature, and connect with our spirituality. But mostly it allows us to simply be ourselves.

Do I take the time to express my creativity today?

THOUGHT FOR THE DAY

I don't have to be a Picasso or a Michelangelo to express my creativity.

PRAYER AND MEDITATION

We can choose from many forms of prayer and meditation to incorporate into our daily lives: silent prayer; following our breath; reading from a religious, inspirational, or spiritual book; worshipping with a group or congregation; and so on. It really doesn't matter which we choose. The important thing is to include it on a regular basis.

If we do, we will discover that we are never alone. In times of fear, loneliness, or stress—as well as during positive times—we will always have something or someone to call on for comfort and strength.

Do I include prayer and meditation in my life today?

THOUGHT FOR THE DAY

*I am never alone when I include
prayer and meditation in my life.*

Hiding behind a Smile

A smile—often unconscious—can represent learned behavior. It can be a defense against what we really think and feel. In pain and turmoil, we may smile and act as if nothing is bothering us. Sometimes this is called "hiding behind a smile."

Perhaps we are trying to fool others; perhaps we are trying to fool ourselves. Either way, it is dishonest.

Today, let us not hide our feelings behind a smile. If we smile today, let our smile be genuine and reflect true happiness.

Do I smile to express, not hide, my true feelings today?

Thought for the Day

A genuine smile both expresses and brings happiness and contentment.

• J U L Y 2 8 •

TRUSTING OURSELVES

For many of us with mental illness, our confidence was torn down somewhere on our journey. Regaining it will be a process.

But with each new day, we can preserve and enhance our self-confidence. Let us trust ourselves and be patient with ourselves on our journey ahead.

Do I practice trusting myself today?

THOUGHT FOR THE DAY

Confidence can always be rebuilt.

COMMUNICATION TAKES COURAGE

Honest, direct communication takes courage, especially for those of us with a mental illness. It seems easier to run from our thoughts and feelings than to share them.

But when we refuse to communicate with others, the results can be devastating. We become prisoners of our illness and life loses meaning.

We start by acknowledging our feelings and then we communicate them to others—one thought at a time, one person at a time, one phone call at a time. We can start saying what is in our minds and our hearts.

Am I isolated and silent today or do I communicate with others and with myself?

THOUGHT FOR THE DAY

*When I find the courage to reach out to others,
I become more alive.*

Becoming Proactive

When we wait for others to call or contact us, we wonder if anyone cares, if anyone knows how we're feeling or understands what we're going through. We wonder where our families and friends are. We wait and wonder: *Why, why won't they call?*

The waiting game can end today. No one can read our mind and know when we are lonely or in need. We are the ones who know, so we are the ones who must reach out to others when we need them or are feeling lonely.

Can I reach out to others today?

Thought for the Day

To get my needs met, I must take the first step.

PURSUING DREAMS

On our journey we may have many dreams. Some will be attainable, some not. But to make any dream come true, we must work for it.

We do this one day at a time, one step at a time, and one breath at a time. To guide us and support us, we have our Higher Power and the people who care about us.

Do I pursue a dream today—knowing that I cannot make it come true by myself?

THOUGHT FOR THE DAY

I pursue my dreams with the support of others and the guidance of my Higher Power.

AUGUST

ACCEPTING OURSELVES

We need not pretend to be anyone or anything we are not. We are who we are. We needn't justify, rationalize, or overcompensate for having an illness any more than for being short or tall, young or old, male or female, black or white.

We live the lives we're given, we do the work we can, and enjoy our friends as they are. We like what we like and we dislike what we dislike. Sometimes we struggle, sometimes we thrive.

We simply are who we are.

Today, can I accept myself for who I am?

THOUGHT FOR THE DAY

Self-acceptance is the essence of recovery.

PRIDE IN OUR PROGRESS

At times we may think we're not making any progress. Because we didn't complete the day's to-do list or put in a full day's work, we think we made no headway.

But whether we run one errand or three, we still made *some* headway. Whether we cleaned one room or four, we still moved forward. Whether we worked two hours or eight, we still made progress. And of this we can feel proud and grateful.

Do I recognize and appreciate my progress today?

THOUGHT FOR THE DAY

*Each achievement is a small success;
falling short of expectations does not mean failure.*

• AUGUST 3 •

LEARNING FROM OUR TROUBLES

Many of us have tried running away from our illness and troubles, only to find that we can't run far enough or fast enough.

But we have a choice. We can keep running or we can try learning from our illness and troubles. They hold value for us, provided we are open-minded and willing.

What can I learn from my illness and troubles today?

THOUGHT FOR THE DAY

The problem itself often holds the key to its resolution.

THE NEWS BLUES

Our outlook may be filled with hope—then we turn on the news and our mood shifts from hopeful to hopeless. For thirty minutes we are bombarded with the world's troubles.

We cannot avoid reality, but we can avoid bombardments of negativity. To remain emotionally and spiritually healthy, we strive for balance between the good and the not so good. Perhaps this means turning off the TV or radio when there's nothing but violence or other bad news.

Today, do I protect my emotions?

THOUGHT FOR THE DAY

I can choose what I let influence me.

Our Support System

When it comes to sharing the fact that we have a mental illness, many of us are reserved. As we should be. It is a medical issue, it is a personal issue, and many people do not understand it.

Yet we need to talk about it. We need emotional and spiritual support on a regular basis. We need practical support in case of an emergency. That's why we develop a network of trusted friends, peers, and professionals we can turn to as needed.

Today, do I have a support system in place to help me deal with my illness?

Thought for the Day

A good support system protects my mental, spiritual, and physical health—and my privacy.

PATIENCE AND FAITH

On our journey, we are certain to have moments when our direction feels unclear or unknown. We may even conclude that our Higher Power has abandoned us.

Sometimes this happens because we're just learning about and accepting our spirituality. Sometimes it's because we have lost patience and faith.

But each of us has a direction. If we remain patient and have faith in our Higher Power and ourselves, the unknown will eventually become known.

Do I have patience and faith today even if my direction is temporarily unknown?

THOUGHT FOR THE DAY

Patience with my Higher Power teaches me that in time, more shall be revealed.

CHALLENGING OUR LIMITS

Life is a gift we receive just once. Yet, for some of us, the gift seems lessened by our illness.

But mental illness does not mean our lives are any less valuable or meaningful. Rather, we make the most of what we have, working within our limits and stretching them as we can. They are only as narrow as we let them be.

As always, we have a choice. Let us begin living our lives to their fullest.

Am I holding myself back or am I living today fully?

THOUGHT FOR THE DAY

To challenge a limit, I expand my thinking
from I can't *to* I'll try *to* I can.

THE WAXING AND WANING OF MENTAL ILLNESS

The symptoms of our illness fade from time to time, but with chronic illnesses they always return. They may go away or lessen for weeks, but will not disappear forever.

It's not clear why our illness won't go away for good or what makes our symptoms change in intensity. But it helps to remember that just as they wax, they also wane.

Today, do I remind myself that feelings are not permanent and that even the worst symptoms eventually improve?

THOUGHT FOR THE DAY

Sometimes recovery has its own timetable.

• A U G U S T   9 •

REASONS TO CARRY ON

At one time or another on our journey, some of us have wanted to quit—to go no further with our lives.

Coping with a mental illness is difficult at best. It is often full of inner pain and turmoil. We can always find reasons to give up.

But despite the pain, with courage and perseverance we can always find one or more reasons to hang on. Whatever they are, let us hold them close.

Do I know my reasons for carrying on today?

THOUGHT FOR THE DAY

I usually have more courage and faith than I give myself credit for.

GRATITUDE FOR MY HIGHER POWER

We sometimes take our Higher Power for granted. It is through recognizing a Power greater than ourselves that we are able to live day by day with our illness and pursue our goals and dreams. Through our Higher Power we learn how to cope with adversity and how to love, as well as how to accept the love of others. We learn the true meaning of self-respect, and believe that we have something to offer others who are in need.

Most of all, we learn that we can be loved and accepted for who we are.

Am I grateful today for the gifts my Higher Power has given me?

THOUGHT FOR THE DAY

The greatest gifts are those that are offered freely and accepted with gratitude.

· A U G U S T 1 1 ·

GETTING THE HELP WE NEED

When our illness flares, some of us may need in-patient care. We may be a danger to ourselves (or others). But the hospital is usually the last place we want to go. Away from home. Confined. We may not trust the doctors or the staff. We may not know when we'll be released and even start to doubt that we're that sick.

Yet through the grace of our Higher Power and the love of family and friends, we get the help we need. Although it can be a difficult time and may take longer than we wish, inpatient care can mean salvation.

If my illness puts me in harm's way today, can I place myself in the hands of people who can care for me?

THOUGHT FOR THE DAY

Sometimes help is at hand
when and where I least expect it.

CLEAN AND SOBER ONE DAY AT A TIME

Staying clean and sober is crucial for those of us with a mental illness. When we mix alcohol or street drugs with our medications, it can be deadly.

One day at a time, we need to do our best to avoid that first drink or fix. And we need to be firm, yet gentle, with ourselves when we fall short of this goal. We are striving for sanity, sobriety, and health.

Do I live a clean and sober lifestyle today?

THOUGHT FOR THE DAY

Nobody ever had a hangover from being high on life.

PROCRASTINATING

Procrastination is a common, intentional behavior that can become habitual. If so, it can become harmful, or even dangerous. When we allow any self-defeating behavior to take over, we are no longer attending to our recovery, our health, or our spiritual life.

To get unstuck, we must begin to change our thinking as well as our behavior. We must begin to face the attitudes and fears that keep us from acting.

Is procrastination an issue in my life today?

THOUGHT FOR THE DAY

*It only takes one step forward
to break the chain of procrastination.*

SHARING OUR DESPAIR

When we hide our despair and refuse to share our feelings with others, they can become deadly secrets. They can eventually turn into thoughts of self-hatred, self-harm, or even suicide.

Most of us hide our feelings because we are afraid of being humiliated. Yet when we let our secrets out, we usually find that they are not as horrible nor as uncommon as we thought. When we open up with people we know and trust, we discover relief and freedom. Best of all, we find solutions to our despair and a measure of peace.

If I have feelings of despair today, do I share them with others?

THOUGHT FOR THE DAY

*Sharing my dark side with people I trust
can be like turning on the light
to prove that a nightmare is not real.*

COPING WITH TRAGEDY

Tragedy is part of life.

We cannot always change the tragedies in our lives, but we do not have to endure our sadness alone. We can seek refuge in our families, our friends, and our Higher Power. No matter how great the tragedy, there is always comfort waiting for us. Let us seek out those who are willing to help and comfort us.

If there is tragedy in my life today, do I allow help from my Higher Power and people who care about me?

THOUGHT FOR THE DAY

*Sometimes it takes a tragedy
to remind me of the caring people
and the presence of a Power in my life.*

WHY ME?

Why me? Why do I have this illness? How long will it last? Will it ever go away? Did I do something to deserve this? Why do I do the things I do? Will I be like this the rest of my life? Will I ever work again? Will I ever be able to hope and dream like other people?

These questions are normal for those of us with a mental illness. But even though we don't always have answers to them, we can move on with our lives. Maybe we will know all the answers one day. But for today, we do our best and know that our Higher Power is with us.

Can I let go of my questions and just live my life today?

THOUGHT FOR THE DAY

Answers to my questions will come if I remain patient.

LOOKING IN THE MIRROR

When we look in the mirror, who is looking back? Is it someone we like or someone we have grown to dislike? Is it someone weak and defective because of illness? Or is it someone good and decent in spite of it?

Ideally we see ourselves for who we are—with strengths and shortcomings, with abilities and limitations. Ideally, we see someone who has grown to accept and love him- or herself (illness and all).

When I look in the mirror today, who do I see looking back?

THOUGHT FOR THE DAY

Accepting my limitations is a sign of health.

ON THE OTHER SIDE OF MY ILLNESS

We no longer have to be a prisoner of our illness. Yes, it is with us day after day, but it doesn't control our every thought and action. We can feel our home is our home, not a prison where hopelessness and despair rule.

Our bed doesn't have to be a place where we hide, but a place where we sleep and dream of things to come. We can live our lives rather than simply survive. We can dare to believe that hopelessness has been transformed into hope, and fear into faith.

We can trust that there is another side to our illness and that through the help of others and our Higher Power, we will find ourselves there.

Do I know the other side of my illness today? If not, can I remind myself that it awaits me?

THOUGHT FOR THE DAY

There is another side to my illness
where peace and freedom await.

KNOWING OUR PURPOSE

Let us never stop believing that we are here for a purpose. We do matter and on our journey we have something to offer.

To find answers, faith, and direction, let us go deeper into our souls. Let us believe in ourselves and never abandon hope.

Do I know what I am living for today?

THOUGHT FOR THE DAY

I am here for a purpose.

• AUGUST 20 •

THOUGHTS AT SUNDOWN

Sometimes a darkness seems to set in, and with it comes the emotional pain. For some of us with mental illness, the darkness becomes a blanket of negativity separating us from rational thinking. Eventually, the darkness can become uncontrollable. Then thoughts of suicide may settle in.

We cannot always avoid these thoughts. But we *can* enlist the help of others, so that thoughts do not become actions. When the sun goes down, we need a plan of action to cope with thoughts and feelings of suicide, so that we will be here to enjoy the promise of tomorrow.

Do I have a safety plan should I feel suicidal? If I begin feeling suicidal today, will I reach out for help?

THOUGHT FOR THE DAY

I can't always control my thoughts but I can choose not to act on them when they give me bad advice.

IS THERE A CURE?

Is there a cure for our illness? Most mental disorders are chronic conditions that will probably be with us for some time to come. Whether for months, years, or decades, we need to learn to live with it.

We had hoped that someone, somewhere would be able to give us the final answer. And someone can. *That someone is us.*

There may not be a cure for our condition as yet, but there is resolution. With practice and patience, we can learn to manage our illness and live with it.

Do I accept responsibility for managing and coping with my illness today?

THOUGHT FOR THE DAY

Accepting and managing my illness
as best I can is my full-time job.

ACCEPTING POWERLESSNESS

It can be frightening to realize that we are powerless over certain aspects of our illness. Most of us felt that once we began taking medications or were introduced to recovery, our powerlessness would disappear. We felt shocked, disappointed, and even betrayed when we realized that this was not the case.

We will likely remain powerless over some aspects of our illness for some time to come. Even with the help of medications, we cannot control every self-defeating behavior or potential relapse that our illness brings about. Yet if we accept this fact, we can let go of what we can't control and manage what we can.

Today, do I know which aspects of my illness I am powerless over and which I can manage?

THOUGHT FOR THE DAY

When I accept my powerlessness,
I can learn to adapt and live with it.

✴

OUR HIGHER POWER IS THERE

We have all done our share of foolish, senseless, and irrational things. Yet through it all, our Higher Power has always been available to us. Our Higher Power is there through our imperfections and foolishness, and continues to accept us in spite of ourselves.

So when we do act foolishly and begin drowning in shame, let us remember that our Higher Power accepts us regardless.

Today, do I know my Higher Power accepts me regardless of what I think or how I feel?

THOUGHT FOR THE DAY

*My Higher Power gives me the best perspective
for how I should see myself.*

MENTAL ILLNESS IS A COMMUNITY AFFAIR

Mental illness is as much a community concern as a personal one. Directly or indirectly, it affects the young, the elderly, family, friends—virtually everyone.

But who is responsible for helping those of us affected by mental illness? Certainly educators, doctors, and counselors can help. But we must not forget about ourselves. We are responsible not just to ourselves, but to the community as a whole. When we speak at a treatment center, lead a support group, or reach out on a personal level, we are accepting this responsibility.

What can I do today to help others or my community?

THOUGHT FOR THE DAY

Although my main responsibility is to myself,
I am also responsible to others and to my community.

LETTING GO

Some of us have let go, while others have not. Some have accepted that we have an illness, while others actively or passively deny it.

Only when we let go of our need to control can we come to accept ourselves and our illness. Only when we stop fighting with ourselves and our illness can we discover that peace and understanding we are searching for.

Have I stopped fighting with myself and my illness today?

THOUGHT FOR THE DAY

*Let my life be directed by acceptance and peace
rather than by fear and control.*

COMPARING OURSELVES TO OTHERS

When we continually compare ourselves to others, we compromise ourselves. We are not giving ourselves enough credit for who we are and for our gifts and talents. And the more we compare ourselves, the less we like ourselves. And the less we like ourselves, the less chance we have to grow.

Do I continually compare myself to others or am I content today with who I am?

THOUGHT FOR THE DAY

Self-acceptance is a first step to change.

• A U G U S T   2 7 •

KILLING THE PAIN WITH ALCOHOL
AND OTHER DRUGS

Some of us have tried to ease our symptoms with alcohol or other drugs. But trying to kill emotional pain doesn't work. We may get temporary relief, but all too soon the pain returns—usually stronger than before. This process can slowly kill us or take us on a journey that ends in insanity.

Instead, let us seek guidance from our friends, our family, trusted professionals, and our Higher Power, to help us find better solutions.

Today, do I simply try to ease my symptoms or do I look for real solutions?

THOUGHT FOR THE DAY

When I use, I am certain to lose.

A Cyclical Illness

Those of use with a mental illness see how it affects the rhythms of our life. Some of us are prone to seasonal worsening of symptoms, while some of us suffer from shorter, repeating patterns. To manage our illness and live our lives to the fullest, we need to learn about the cycles of our illness, pay attention to them, and plan accordingly.

Do I know where I am in my cycle today?

Thought for the Day

My illness can be my wisest teacher.

PRIVILEGED PEOPLE

Let us celebrate the times when we have risen from despair and are now managing our illness and moving on with our lives. We know then that we have abilities and dreams for our future. We can establish relationships and we can help others in times of need. We are given a second chance at life. For all of this, we are grateful.

Do I realize that I am one of the privileged today?

THOUGHT FOR THE DAY

It is the greatest of privileges to be alive, in recovery, and in the care of my Higher Power.

OPENING OUR WINGS

At times we hope for happiness like a bird just sitting in a tree, waiting for the next meal. We do nothing and hope happiness will just come flying our way.

Yet every day offers us the possibility of happiness. Let us open our wings and fly. The more we open ourselves to new possibilities, the more likely we are to find happiness.

Today, do I remain alert and open?

THOUGHT FOR THE DAY

I can't find happiness if I don't look for it.

Our Painful and Confusing Past

Driven to despair and hopelessness, some of us with mental illness have tried harming ourselves or others. Thankfully—and through the grace of our Higher Power—we survived those painful and confusing times.

But do we allow ourselves to remember the details of those times? Or have we tried to close the door? As painful as it may be to recall these events, we need to do so, for they can be our guide in preventing a recurrence.

Fortunately, we do not have to make this journey alone. There are others who can guide us and comfort us through this process—but we must ask for their help.

With the help of others who care, am I willing to accept my past and examine it today without shame, blame, or despair?

Thought for the Day

*Though painful, uncovering my past
will help me recover.*

SEPTEMBER

EVEN WHEN WE'RE BLUE

When we are feeling down and lonely, or when our illness is acting up, it's easy to think that no one loves us. We're miserable. We don't love ourselves. Why would anyone else?

We may not always realize it, but there are family members and friends who still love us when we're blue, even when our illness is acting up—in fact, *especially* then.

Today, do I realize that there are others who love and care for me, even when I'm blue?

THOUGHT FOR THE DAY

People who really accept me, also accept my illness.

• S E P T E M B E R   2 •

FACING REALITY

When life becomes hard to bear, we may not want to live in the real world. We may prefer to retreat into *our own* world, where we feel safe, where there are no unbearable situations, and where we make all the rules.

But this world is not real. Comforting as it may seem, it is actually a world of isolation, pain, and self-destruction. In fact, it is where our illness rules and where we become a prisoner.

We may not like what life brings us today, but we need to face it as best we can.

Do I face reality today even if my situation is hard to bear?

THOUGHT FOR THE DAY

Mental health means dealing with what is real.

ILLNESS MEANS CHANGE

Having a mental illness, like any illness, suggests that we need to change something in our lives. Chances are we are stuck in an unhealthy direction or attitude. We need to put one foot in front of the other and begin to take risks. The possibilities are endless.

What am I willing to change today?

THOUGHT FOR THE DAY

The result of illness can be change and growth.

RESTLESS AND RECKLESS

For some of us, feeling restless can make us reckless. If we grow restless and fail to turn to our Higher Power, we may get reckless. Our decisions will become less rational and our behavior will get out of control. Our lives may be endangered.

To prevent this dangerous recklessness, we need to identify and cope with the thoughts and feelings that lead to it. We must not avoid them or pretend they aren't there. Instead, we need to accept them and any pain they bring. If necessary, we ask for help.

Am I alert to any restlessness today?

THOUGHT FOR THE DAY

To stay safe, I need to stay alert to my warning signs.

• SEPTEMBER 5 •

TOO MANY PROBLEMS

When we have too many of yesterday's, today's, and tomorrow's problems on our mind, we're headed for trouble. If we don't let go of our worry and our attachment to certain outcomes, we may suffer an emotional, physical, or spiritual breakdown.

We can handle only so much stress at one time. Eventually, we need to let go and let our Higher Power and others help us. When we do this, we are on the road to relief and serenity.

If I have too many problems on my mind today, do I offer them up to my Higher Power?

THOUGHT FOR THE DAY

Focusing only on problems, and trying to deal with them entirely on my own, only creates bigger problems.

WANTING SOMETHING DIFFERENT

Some of us may feel that we are in a rut. Our life is the same day after day. We live from crisis to crisis. We feel limited by our illness. Yet we feel powerless to take a new direction.

Our life can change. But first we must be willing to *do* something different. With faith and a willingness to work, the story can change.

Is today the start of a new chapter—or a brand new story—in my life?

THOUGHT FOR THE DAY

I can reclaim my life—one day at a time.

SETTING BOUNDARIES

Setting boundaries means knowing when to say yes and when to say no. Our boundaries must match our behavior, and what we do must match what we say. If we set a boundary and don't stick to it, the boundary is useless.

When we first begin setting healthy boundaries, others may object, and we may feel uncomfortable or even guilty. It can be hard to tell someone no and stick to it. But we can learn to do it because we know that letting others control or manipulate us undermines our recovery. The more we practice setting healthy boundaries and sticking to them, the easier it becomes.

Do I set healthy boundaries today?

THOUGHT FOR THE DAY

Healthy boundaries promote healthy relationships.

MEDICATIONS AND SEX

Some medications for mental illness can have a powerful effect on our sexuality, both on desire and physical capability. As a result, some of us may conclude that we're defective. But it's the medication, not us. We need not blame ourselves for what is not our fault at all. Some of us may even conclude that taking medication is no longer worth it and quit. But then our symptoms return and may even worsen.

Let us remember that if we quit taking the very medication that helps us, our chances of recovery will worsen; let us remember that side effects are not a personal shortcoming.

If medication impairs my sexuality, can I accept the change for today?

THOUGHT FOR THE DAY

Taking medication is a sign of recovery.

HIDING

Many of us with a mental illness know all too well what it is like to hide in the darkness of night. We know the comfort it can bring. For many of us, darkness is a friend, never judging or questioning us. It may have embarrassed us, but it has never failed us.

Yet how long can we keep hiding before it consumes us? How long before our friend becomes our enemy?

Today, as darkness approaches, let us not hide within it. Today, let us look for new ways of coping with our feelings and our illness.

Do I retreat into darkness and isolation today or do I seek the companionship of caring people?

THOUGHT FOR THE DAY

I can cope with my illness and grow to love myself if I reach out to others.

LEARNING FROM THE PAST

How many times have we told ourselves, *I'm never going to do that again?* Yet even when we know the harmful consequences of our behavior, we do it over and over again.

If the consequences of that road are harmful, then it's time to take a new road. It's time to start asking others for their opinions and asking for guidance from our Higher Power. It is time to begin learning from the choices we make.

Do I take the same well-worn road today or do I learn from past experience?

THOUGHT FOR THE DAY

*The road I have not yet traveled
may be the healthiest road for me.*

Worthy of Love

At one time or another, many of us with mental illness felt that we were no longer worthy of love.

Not so. All of us—no matter how sick—deserve to be loved.

The problem for many of us is what we tell ourselves. It helps if we can avoid the negative self-talk. It helps if we can simply remind ourselves that we deserve to be loved. And it helps to recognize that being loved starts with loving ourselves.

Today, can I remind myself that I am worthy of love?

Thought for the Day

*If I don't love myself, it may be
hard to know that I am loved.*

SIMPLY A CHRONIC ILLNESS

It is not our fault that we have a mental illness. We have done nothing to deserve it. It is a biological illness like diabetes, cancer, and so on.

But as with any chronic illness, we need to cope with it. When we follow a well-guided plan, our chances for recovery increase. We do what is necessary to manage our illness, as well as our emotional, physical, and spiritual health.

Having a mental illness does not mean we are sentenced to a life of pain and misery. Millions like us thrive on their journeys. And so can we.

Am I doing what is necessary to support my recovery today?

THOUGHT FOR THE DAY

Each mental illness has its own set of symptoms and its own set of solutions.

COURAGE TO STAND

At one time or another, we have all tried running away from ourselves and our illness, only to find both waiting for us when we returned. It didn't matter how fast, how far, or which direction we ran. We could not get away from our troubles, our illness, ourselves.

Eventually we must face what we are running from and what lies within. Perhaps not today or tomorrow or next week, but eventually.

Can I face my illness today and what lies within?

THOUGHT FOR THE DAY

The foundation of my recovery is finding the courage to stand and face myself.

BEING ASSERTIVE

Being assertive is not the same as being aggressive. Being aggressive means being demanding and forceful. This type of behavior rarely works. In fact, it often creates fear and avoidance.

Being assertive, on the other hand, means being direct, yet honest and respectful.

Let us remember that we stand a far better chance of getting our wants and needs met when we are calm and assertive, rather than agitated and aggressive.

Am I aggressive or am I assertive today?

THOUGHT FOR THE DAY

To get my wants and needs met,
I am neither aggressive nor passive, but assertive.

WHEN OUR RESPONSIBILITIES
BECOME OUR ENEMY

We all have responsibilities. Some we like and some we don't like. Some are higher on our priority list than others.

If we're not careful, however, responsibilities and commitments can become wearisome, frightening, or even paralyzing. When too great and too numerous, they become our enemies.

Let us be realistic about what we are able to do. Let us put aside our pride and use our wisdom when we take on responsibilities. And let us learn to say no when we need to.

Today, do I accept my responsibilities and make commitments in a healthy way?

THOUGHT FOR THE DAY

I can only do so much in one day.

EXPECTING THE WORST

Some of us have grown used to expecting the worst to happen in our lives. Why not? Pieces of our lives have been taken away; we have experienced powerlessness and hopelessness.

Yet by always expecting the worst to happen, we may overlook possibilities for making things better or miss the good things when they come along.

Just because we have a mental illness does not mean we are cursed.

Today, do I expect the worst or do I stay open to the good things?

THOUGHT FOR THE DAY

I'm more likely to notice the good things in my life when I keep a positive attitude.

FINDING OURSELVES

For most of us with a mental illness, the journey has not been easy. We've had highs and lows. We've been lost and we've been found. We have known peace and despair. But now that we are in recovery, things are more likely to start settling down.

Yet some of us aren't quite sure who we are or where we belong in the world.

This make sense. Mental illness is highly disruptive. The good news is that answers will come. Only it will take time. In recovery we are still growing and growth can't be forced.

Today, can I practice patience and use all the tools of recovery?

THOUGHT FOR THE DAY

Sometimes it's when I stop working so hard to find myself, that I find what I am looking for.

REMEMBERING

There are some events in our lives that we would like to forget, especially those surrounding our illness. There are the relapses, the broken relationships, and perhaps suicidal thoughts. But however painful it may be to recall them, they are part of us.

When we face our past and our illness, we can learn many lessons and gain much wisdom. When we accept who we are and where we have come from, the power shifts in our favor. What we once feared is no longer our enemy but a source of wisdom, and a signpost that points to who we truly want to be.

Today, do I remember where I have come from?

THOUGHT FOR THE DAY

My past can be my guide for the journey ahead.

GETTING ANGRY

There are times when we may come to the conclusion that because we have a mental illness and our lives have been altered without our permission, it is okay to mistreat others or try to make them feel as bad as we do. But this is not okay. Those of us with a mental illness have every right to be angry, but we have no right to harm others just because we are hurting.

If we do get angry at someone, we are obliged to step back and see whether our anger is legitimate and appropriate. If it is, then and only then should we tell them clearly that we are angry at them and why. If it isn't, we need to make amends as soon as we can.

Today, if I get angry, can I express it appropriately?

THOUGHT FOR THE DAY

*It is important to treat others
the way I want to be treated.*

CHOOSING HOPE

We will never know the hundreds of people whose faces and names appear on those billboards, reminding us that depression and other forms of mental illness can take one's life.

For those people it is too late for recovery. But not for us. We have today. We have choices. We can choose to have hope. We can have faith in the future, in our Higher Power, and in ourselves. When we begin feeling as if there is no hope, let us reach out to others. Let us not become a name and a face on a billboard.

If I feel despair or hopelessness today, will I turn to others for help?

THOUGHT FOR THE DAY

I have choices and I can choose hope.

PRAYING IN THE MORNING

Before starting our day, we can relax a moment and think of the twenty-four hours that lie ahead. We can ask our Higher Power for the strength to manage our illness. We can ask for the patience to live within any of our limitations. We can ask our Higher Power to help us grow spiritually and emotionally. But, most of all, we can thank our Higher Power that we have another day.

Have I communed with my Higher Power today?

THOUGHT FOR THE DAY

Prayer can improve my life and help me
be less self-centered.

VALUING OUR LIVES

What value do we place on our lives today? Do we feel we have something to offer others? Do we feel we have a purpose? Do we feel that we belong in the world, and that a part of the world is in us?

Our lives hold whatever value we place on them. They can be meaningful or empty. The choice is ours.

What value do I place on my life today?

THOUGHT FOR THE DAY

When I hold my life in contempt, I am diminished;
when I value my life, it is enhanced
and I live my life fully.

AMAZING

We are truly amazing! We have risen to our feet again and again. We have faced down our illness with courage, faith, and determination. Perhaps we have found peace and acceptance.

Over the months or years of coping with our illness, we have discovered that it no longer has to be our enemy. We have discovered that it does not define us. We have persevered in working toward our goals and dreams each day and we have accomplished some amazing things.

Today, do I realize just how amazing I am?

THOUGHT FOR THE DAY

Despite my illness, I can lead a full, successful, and rewarding life.

TURNING TO MY HIGHER POWER

We can turn to our Higher Power now to help us meet our needs and goals. We can ask for good health, so that we can carry on our work each day. We can seek to stay strong so that we can cope with our illness, one day at a time.

We can look for support as we strive to be kind, unselfish, and attentive to the needs of others. And if sickness or accident befall us, we reach out.

When we're feeling lonely or in despair, we ask our Higher Power to lift our head and heart so that we can move forward with courage.

Do I know my Higher Power is available to me today, even when I am alone?

THOUGHT FOR THE DAY

No matter what my illness may tell me,
I need never be truly alone.

SHARING OUR WISDOM AND EXPERIENCE

Some of us have successfully managed our illness for months or years. On our journey we have learned a great deal from trial and error and from others' wisdom and experience.

But many are just beginning their journey with mental illness. They may seek our help. They will want to know what we have learned and they may come to us thirsty for knowledge. Let us be helpful and generous with what we have learned.

Do I share my wisdom and experience with others today?

THOUGHT FOR THE DAY

*Sharing my wisdom and experience with others
strengthens me and reminds me
of how far I have come.*

HEALTHY WORK

Some of us with mental illness can work forty hours a week, some only part-time. We do only what we are capable of doing. We don't compete with others. We do what is best in each situation.

If our illness tells us not to go to work, we assess the situation and do what we can to go; but if our illness has taken control of us and working is not possible, we let the right people know. Then we do what is necessary to care for ourselves and survive the day outside of work.

We do everything we can to be a good worker, but recovery comes first and we do what is best in each situation.

Do I take a healthy approach to work today?

THOUGHT FOR THE DAY

My work should not contribute to my illness.

PEACE AND CONTENTMENT

Society wants us to believe that money can take away our pain and problems. We hear this message every day.

Looking back on our lives, sometimes we've had money and sometimes we haven't. Yet we still had pain and problems.

In short, peace and contentment can come only from within.

Today, do I look to my heart and Higher Power for what is most important in life?

THOUGHT FOR THE DAY

Peace and contentment can be mine—
because it always comes from within.

TRUTH IS AN ESSENTIAL

When we have a setback, or when our illness has taken hold of us, we must admit it to ourselves and, when necessary, to others.

Some of us may be tempted to try to fool others (or ourselves) into believing that everything is fine. We don't want to admit that we have taken a step back. But by not admitting what has happened—or what may be happening right now—we allow our fear and pride to control us. We put our physical, emotional, and spiritual lives in danger.

Setbacks are normal from time to time. They do not make us weaker or less-valued. When we feel tempted to deny our situation, let us cast aside our fear and pride and admit that we are having trouble. That way we can get whatever help we need. We can move forward.

If I have a setback today, will I admit it?

THOUGHT FOR THE DAY

Truth is essential to recovery.

WE ARE NOT ALONE

When our illness took control of us in the past, we probably acted in ways we're not proud of. This is to be expected. Yet some of us may believe that what we did was unforgivable. As a result, we condemn ourselves to lives of guilt and shame.

Whatever we did, we're not the first to do it. This does not excuse our behavior. But it helps to know that someone, somewhere, has done what we have done. It helps to know that we are not alone in our struggles and do not deserve a life of guilt and shame.

Today, do I realize that I can make amends and recover my life, no matter what I've done?

THOUGHT FOR THE DAY

Recovery is easier with company.

ACCEPTANCE

Until we come to accept just who we are and the fact that we have an illness, our life will involve constant battling and bargaining with our Higher Power.

But this rarely gets us what we really want or need. It just makes our situation worse and we become more confused and resentful.

Yet when we accept who we are and the fact that we have an illness, we no longer need to battle and bargain.

Do I accept my life today?

THOUGHT FOR THE DAY

With acceptance and faith come hope and options.

OCTOBER

FACING FEARS

Many of us know what it is like to endure the darkness of night. Seconds turn into hours and minutes into days. We know the night can fill our rational minds with irrational and uncontrollable thoughts.

But just as our mind can shift from stability to irrationality, it can shift back. Nights can become a time to rejuvenate, rather than fear. To take back the night, we face our fears, our loneliness, and whatever night brings.

Can I begin today to face the parts of me that emerge when darkness falls?

THOUGHT FOR THE DAY

To take back what belongs to me, I move forward with faith and courage despite my fears.

· O C T O B E R   2 ·

How We Look at the World

The world we live in has much that is good and much that is bad. Each day we can seek out the positive or the negative. If we choose to dwell on the negative, then that is what we will experience. But if we dwell on the positive, then that is more likely what we will experience.

The choice today is ours. We are the only ones who have the power to change how we look at the world.

How do I view the world today?

Thought for the Day

*It is remarkable how things change
when I decide to change the way I look at them*

Adjusting Our Medication

Many of us with a mental illness will change medication or dosages as our illness warrants. And for some of us, these changes can bring about temporary turmoil: thoughts and feelings change rapidly, stimulating confusion or fear.

Should this happen, it is important not to panic and lose faith in the medications. Usually this period of instability will pass; it is worth the effort. If it doesn't pass in a reasonable amount of time, then we seek professional help and make the proper adjustments.

Throughout this process, let us remember that we don't have to endure this process alone. There are others who have been where we are today, and who are willing to support us.

Today, do I remember that adjusting medication is a process, that it will end, and that I can endure it with the help of others?

Thought for the Day

*Having support is important
when making important changes.*

✳

RECOVERY FIRST

Money and possessions are not harmful, but how we go about obtaining them can be. If we decide that wealth is more important than our health and recovery, then we have a problem.

We can achieve many things, but not by sacrificing ourselves in the process. What we need is a sense of balance. If we have not learned that recovery must come first, we may lose what we have.

Today, do I place my health, my recovery, and coping with my illness first in my life?

THOUGHT FOR THE DAY

My desires tend to get simpler as I get healthier.

· OCTOBER 5 ·

LOST IN THE FUTURE

Some of us spend so much time dreaming about what might be, that today comes and goes without our noticing it. We are caught up in careers, hopes, and worries—and forget about living in today.

Instead of getting lost in our mental future, let us strive for a healthy balance. Instead of letting our thoughts control us, let us set aside time each day to ponder and plan. The rest of the time we stick to the here and now.

Today, am I living in the here and now?

THOUGHT FOR THE DAY

Those who live in the future cannot enjoy today.

HEALTHY PLEASURE

Many of us put off doing the things we don't want to do. But some of us even put off doing the healthy, pleasurable things we *want* to do. Perhaps they are new or seem risky to us.

Today is a good day to break that pattern. Life is short. Let us pick a healthy, pleasurable thing we've wanted to do and just do it!

Today, do I do at least one healthy, pleasurable thing I have been wanting to do?

THOUGHT FOR THE DAY

Fostering happiness and satisfaction
promotes my recovery.

Avoiding Overloads

An overload of stress—whether it hits all at once or builds up slowly—can throw our emotions and symptoms into a tailspin. We can become depressed or isolated, or manic and unpredictable.

To avoid becoming a volcano, we must learn to avoid stress. To avoid a situation that is painful and dangerous to ourselves, to others, or both, we must learn to cope with the unavoidable stress. To do both, we must be willing to ask others for help.

Do I manage the stresses in my life today?

Thought for the Day

When stress builds up, it's time to reach out for help.

AVOIDING SHAME

At times we tend to self-destruct by staying stuck in our shame. We enter that part of our world where our shame and guilt are lurking. We push our special button—or have it pushed for us—and wait for the shame and guilt to surface and take control.

But we can learn to live another way. Rather than giving in to our shame, we can learn to confront and cope with the issues that cause it. We can then begin to open the door to self-love and acceptance.

Today, do I examine what is behind my shame, instead of giving in to it?

THOUGHT FOR THE DAY

If shame and guilt help me self-destruct,
acceptance helps me grow and recover.

THE BREAKFAST CLUB

For some of us, there is a "Breakfast Club," a group of people we have grown to love as family, the ones we depend on for support, day after day and week after week. They are the ones with whom we share our souls and from whom we gain wisdom; the ones who accept us and our illness without condition.

On our journey we need friendships like these. Life can be difficult for those of us with a mental illness and we cannot go it alone.

Do I have friendships and a support system that I can depend on today?

THOUGHT FOR THE DAY

Deep and abiding friendships are important
for my journey.

Every Moment Is Precious

We have a second chance in the wake of our illness—a chance at a new life, a new journey. An opportunity to know ourselves as never before. An opportunity to make our hopes and dreams come true.

Each moment is precious. It can and should be lived to its fullest. This is our task, every moment of every day.

Today, do I make the most of what has been given to me?

Thought for the Day

*Being present helps me make the most
of every moment.*

STANDING APART FROM LOVE

Just because we have a mental illness doesn't mean we are unlovable or can't be in a healthy relationship. After all, having a chemical imbalance doesn't mean we lack feelings or are unable to love.

If we are standing apart from love because of our illness, then we do ourselves and others an injustice. We are denying ourselves—and the people who care about us—one of the greatest gifts of all.

Do I withhold love from myself and others today or do I allow myself to feel and express it?

THOUGHT FOR THE DAY

I am much more than my illness.

SINGLE-HANDED RECOVERY

When we feel better and our lives are in order, we may think we no longer need help. If so, we have reached the dangerous point of single-handed recovery.

At those times it is important to keep in mind that we are not cured and that we don't know all there is to know about living day by day. If we remain alone and act as though we know best, single-handed recovery is bound to lead to self-defeat and perhaps back to the beginning of our recovery.

We need to remember that others are willing to guide us emotionally, spiritually, and physically, and that there will be times when we need to let them. We might also remember that, at every moment, we can look to our Higher Power.

Do I rule my recovery today or do I let others help me?

THOUGHT FOR THE DAY

To walk alone can be a lonely and confusing journey; to walk with many is to be strong and united.

❈

POSITIVE MESSAGES

At one time or another, many of us with mental illness have said, *I don't care anymore. I can't stand living with this illness anymore. I'm never going to get any better.* Usually this tape plays in our minds when our illness acts up, when our lives aren't going well, or when things seem out of control.

The good news is that we can replace this tape with a positive message. We can remind ourselves of how things really are, using messages such as *I will get better, I'm not alone, I can learn to cope with my illness, I can get through this moment, I can rely on my Higher Power,* and so on. With practice, we can do this as often as necessary to get ourselves through the rough times.

What mental tapes will I play today if I begin to stop caring?

THOUGHT FOR THE DAY

With positive but realistic thinking, I can make it through rough times.

❋

Obsessive Behavior

Obsessive thoughts and behaviors are symptoms of many types of mental illness. They can be about drugs, alcohol, sex, food, self-destructive behaviors, people, or places. Obsessions can be harmless or they can be deadly.

But even when the most powerful obsessive thoughts overtake us, we can still unhook from them. We can write them on paper, we can share them by phone with someone, and we can ask our Higher Power to help. If necessary, we can get in touch with a professional or a crisis center.

If I have obsessive thoughts today, will I let them keep me prisoner or will I act to release myself from them?

Thought for the Day

I can find release from my obsessions by reaching out.

Reasonable Risks

From time to time, many of us felt sure we would never be able to live with our illness. Yet, today, here we are: alive and doing things to manage our illness.

To get here, we had to take some risks. We didn't know whether this new way or that new way would work. But we took a leap—and many of the things we tried did work!

Still, many of us are afraid to take risks in recovery because we are afraid of the unknown. We are not sure what will give us relief. But there is one thing we do know: if we don't begin taking risks today, we won't make progress and we may begin slipping backwards.

Do I take reasonable risks today when it comes to managing my illness?

Thought for the Day

Taking reasonable risks can change my life.

FEELING SORRY FOR OURSELVES

Sometimes we may think, *Considering what we have endured on our journey, we have every right to feel sorry for ourselves. For that matter, everyone else should feel sorry for us, too.*

But where does a "poor me" attitude lead us? It leads to resentment and self-destruction. It leads us to isolation, loneliness, and ultimately, despair. We end up where it is harder for people to understand us and care about us. It is a place of hopelessness.

It is natural and even healthy to feel sorry for ourselves from time to time. But if we allow self-pity to guide our thoughts and actions, we can damage ourselves.

Today, am I grateful for my life?

THOUGHT FOR THE DAY

I can learn to accept and appreciate life by looking for gratitude and solutions.

✳

No Quick Fixes

Some of us with mental illness are convinced that someone, somewhere, has a quick and easy cure for us.

But chances are, we're in for disappointment. There are usually no complete cures or quick fixes. There are only day-by-day solutions, solutions that will help us cope with our illness and break free of unfulfilled expectations.

When we accept the fact that there are no quick fixes nor complete cures for now, we are ready and able to put the many day-by-day solutions into practice.

Am I looking for quick and easy answers today or am I applying solutions?

Thought for the Day

Day-by-day solutions help me cope.

FEELING DESPERATE

Desperation may be familiar to those of us with mental illness. We know how it feels to want to get out of bed, yet be unable to move. We know how it feels to want to control our thoughts and actions, yet be unable to. We know how it feels to look for understanding, yet not get it. Worst of all, we know how it feels to want to live, yet at the same time want to die.

The opposite of desperation is serenity. We can find it through our Higher Power, through our friends, through others who genuinely care about us, and sometimes through professionals.

When we are feeling desperate, we need to reach out to others and to our Higher Power. When we do this, we take that all-important first step toward serenity.

If I start to feel desperate today, do I remember to reach out and take that first step toward serenity?

THOUGHT FOR THE DAY

I can move from desperation to serenity.

✺

RECOVERING

When recovering from a bout of serious illness, we must avoid trying to put our lives back in order too quickly. Chances are, we have been bruised emotionally, spiritually, and perhaps even physically by our illness. (We may have bruised others as well.) We need to be patient and gentle with ourselves as we regain our footing and find the path of recovery once again.

Recovering takes energy, will, and patience. Trying to hurry may set us up for disaster.

It is important to remember that some of us will recover faster than others. But this is not a race. Our job is to put our lives back together, one piece at a time.

Have I learned not to hurry my recovery today, while remaining fully committed to it?

THOUGHT FOR THE DAY

When recuperating, it is important to be realistic.

✳

RECURRING ILLNESS

The fear of our illness coming back and taking control haunts many us. It is common and natural. But for some of us, this fear runs our lives.

Yet we can let go of this fear and live lives of trust and hope. We will not lose it overnight. But each time we make it through a setback, we will be that much stronger and wiser. We will know better how to cope the next time. And as we learn, we become more hopeful, more successful in our recovery, and less afraid.

If fear of my illness arises today, can I practice letting it go and trusting my Higher Power?

THOUGHT FOR THE DAY

*With patience and persistence, fear can be
transformed into trust and hope.*

GONE BUT NOT FORGOTTEN

Many people with mental illness have lost their lives to it. But they are not to be forgotten. They have shown us what it is like to struggle. They have shown us what to do and what not to do.

As we walk on our journey, let us respectfully remember those who are no longer with us, and take what wisdom we can from their lives.

Today, can I learn from those who have gone before me?

THOUGHT FOR THE DAY

Experience is invaluable in recovering from illness.

EMOTIONALLY WOUNDED

How do we respond when we are emotionally wounded? Do we attack? Do we get angry or resentful? Do we turn inward and hate ourselves? Do we isolate ourselves? Or do we bring our true feelings to light and seek healing with others' help?

On our journey, we are sure to get wounded from time to time. How we cope makes a difference.

How will I respond if I am emotionally wounded today?

THOUGHT FOR THE DAY

I can choose how I cope.
Healthy choices promote growth.

Losing Concentration

Having difficulty concentrating is common for those of us with a mental illness. It can be frustrating, crippling, or even paralyzing. Some of us have even given up medications in the hope of improving concentration.

If we are having difficulty concentrating, the first thing we need to do is admit this to ourselves. Next, we remind ourselves that we're no less of a person because of it.

Then, to improve our concentration, we put forth some effort, gently. If our medications are the cause, we may see if an adjustment will help. We are learning to accept progress, rather than insisting on perfection.

Today, am I gentle with myself if I have difficulty concentrating?

Thought for the Day

Perfect concentration is impossible,
but it can be improved, gently and gradually.

✳

ASKING FOR HELP

Mental illness can turn a balanced life into one of loneliness and despair.

Yet mental illness is not without hope. It is treatable and manageable. Our emotional balance can be restored. Our hopelessness can be relieved. Our desire and will to go on living can be revived, *provided we ask for help*.

Today, do I remember to ask for help when I need it?

THOUGHT FOR THE DAY

With every mental illness there is hope and healing, with help.

CLEAR THINKING

If we think there is no way out and all seems hopeless, we may not be thinking clearly.

If we begin contemplating suicide, let's not forget that it is an irreversible move.

Before we decide that there is no way out, it is critical that we reach out to friends, family members, and professionals. Better yet, let us decide that suicide is not an option.

Do I choose life today?

THOUGHT FOR THE DAY

Good decisions require clear thinking.

RED LIGHT, GREEN LIGHT

In our recovery, we will sometimes get a green light to proceed with an action or decision. Sometimes, we will get a red light to stop for a time, take stock, and rest. At still other times, we may be unsure which light is shining.

We need to learn to distinguish which light is shining, when we should proceed, and when we should stop. If we're not sure, friends, family, professionals, or our Higher Power can all help. We are not alone and we do not have to make difficult decisions on our own.

Today, do I observe my situation carefully to see whether a green or red light is shining? If I can't tell, will I ask others I trust for help?

THOUGHT FOR THE DAY

Wisdom is knowing when to move forward,
when to stay put, and when to ask for help.

WRITING OUR OWN SCRIPT

In recovery we are given a second chance, an opportunity to begin a new journey. We have the chance to write part of our own script, to help shape our life in the direction we would like it to go. Only two writers can decide our destiny: ourselves and our Higher Power. Together we write our script and act it out.

Yet many of us turn away from this chance. We are afraid and retreat to safer, familiar places rather than take a path into the unknown.

Today, will I retreat from the unknown or work together with my Higher Power?

THOUGHT FOR THE DAY

I can help shape the life I want to live.

GETTING ADVICE

Some people know more about us, our illness, and its symptoms than we do. Usually these people are family members, friends, and professionals. All can help guide us every day with the wisdom of their experience. They won't always be right, of course. And we shouldn't do what they suggest automatically, simply because they say so. But because they care about us, what they say is worth listening to and considering carefully.

Some of us, however, remain stubborn, thinking we have all the answers and disregarding the people who care about us. Taking advice is difficult for all of us at times, but this kind of thinking can lead to danger and undermine our recovery.

Today, do think I have all the answers or do I listen to others?

THOUGHT FOR THE DAY

Listening to others can be a way of trusting in a Power greater than ourselves.

MONITORING SAD

Many of us with mental illness experience some degree of seasonal affective disorder (also called SAD). For most of us, it comes during the darkest months; for some, the brightest.

These months have proven dangerous for those of us with mental illness, a time when our emotions can run astray. It helps to remind ourselves that we have an illness and that this illness may give us dangerous or even deadly messages. During this time, we carefully monitor and manage our thoughts, feelings, and actions.

Do I take care of myself today by carefully monitoring my thoughts, feelings, and actions?

THOUGHT FOR THE DAY

*I pay attention to the cycles of my illness,
but especially my seasonal cycle.*

CHECKING IN

It's important to let others know just how we're do-ing. Whether we're feeling good or bad, up or down, it helps to check in. It maintains our connection with those close to us and keeps us from isolating ourselves.

We can talk about what's going on in our lives, and then listen when they tell us about their lives. In this way, we can help keep our illness from taking over.

But in order for this to happen, we must be willing to do our part and pay a visit or pick up the phone sometimes.

Will I check in with others today?

THOUGHT FOR THE DAY

*Letting others know how I am doing
is a sign of good mental health.*

TRICK OR TREAT?

Some of us have come to believe that our mental illness has made our life journey one big trick. Yet recovery is one of the greatest gifts we will ever receive. The only trick is the one we play on ourselves when we don't believe recovery is possible for us.

We trick ourselves when we fail to live one day at a time, stay in the here and now, and embrace what our recovery offers us. We trick ourselves when we feel sorry for ourselves and focus on what we think we ought to have instead of what we do have.

But when we remain true to ourselves, our recovery, and our journey, we discover that our recovery is entirely a treat.

Today, do I realize that my recovery is a treat and a gift?

THOUGHT FOR THE DAY

The treats in store for me in recovery
are there when I am ready to receive them.

❋

NOVEMBER

THE LATCH ON THE DOOR

Often when our illness takes hold and the need for isolation overwhelms us, some of us may retreat behind a locked door. For a time, isolation can relieve our problems and we feel safe. But eventually, our problems will follow us into the room. The lock cannot keep the illness outside.

When we feel like withdrawing, we reach out to others for help.

If the desire for isolation becomes strong today, do I first reach out to others?

THOUGHT FOR THE DAY

The more I connect with others,
the less I need to isolate.

FRUSTRATION

Coping with mental illness is certain to lead to some frustrating moments. At times it can feel like threading a needle. The first few misses are expected. But when the misses pile up and the frustration shows, we may be tempted to give up.

If we want serenity in our recovery, however, we can't let frustration rule our thinking and behavior. We can't give up because of near misses.

Few things we do, especially at first, turn out perfectly. Persistence, patience, tolerance, self-love, and even frustration are useful watchwords if we are to achieve and sustain serenity in our recovery.

Do I cope wisely and patiently with frustration today?

THOUGHT FOR THE DAY

Frustration can teach me patience.

· N O V E M B E R 3 ·

GUILT

When our illness had control of our lives, it dictated every thought and action. Our ways were self-centered and self-seeking. We may have harmed ourselves. We may have harmed others, though we did not intend to.

As time passed, some of us have become overwhelmed with guilt. We could not face ourselves nor anyone from our past. Guilt was dictating our thoughts, feelings, and actions.

But we can let go of the guilt we've been carrying around. We can make amends as best we can to the people we have harmed. We can say, "I'm sorry. What I did was wrong." We can explain our illness to them without making excuses. We can make better choices in the future. We can take care to avoid repeating the situations that led to our harming others.

Today, do I make amends if possible and loosen my grip on guilt?

THOUGHT FOR THE DAY

Amends bring peace.

WITH TRUTH COMES PEACE

If we feel we are defective, we may try to compensate. We may strive compulsively to be perfect in other areas of our life. Sometimes this move is unconscious and sometimes it is purposeful. Yet no human being is perfect.

We cannot hide from our imperfections and expect to find and maintain peace within. Only truth brings about acceptance and peace.

Today, do I seek truth and accept myself as I am?

THOUGHT FOR THE DAY

I am perfectly imperfect.

BEING HONEST

Many of us know well what it is like to hide our thoughts and feelings from our family members, partner, or spouse—particularly when it comes to our illness and its symptoms. Some of us feel embarrassed, while others fear a reaction.

Yet when we hide these thoughts and feelings from the person we are closest to, we create a make-believe relationship.

To be true to ourselves and the people we care about, we must become honest and communicate as best we can. We must take a risk. We must begin to reveal, step by step and day by day, what is within us.

Today, do I hide the real me or do I share what is within?

THOUGHT FOR THE DAY

Dishonesty separates me from myself and others.

LIVING A FULL LIFE

Many of us still fear at times that our illness will keep us prisoner forever, that our lives are over. We might surface periodically, only to see the world passing us by.

But we're finding now that recovery brings us strength. We can no longer just let our lives pass us by. Our desire for life is growing, and we are breaking the chains that once imprisoned us.

Am I living today fully?

THOUGHT FOR THE DAY

When times are toughest, I can still believe that every moment of life is precious.

NAGGING THOUGHTS

We all have unsettling or disturbing thoughts in the back of our mind. Some thoughts may be confusing but harmless, while others may be dangerous. At times these thoughts can scare us—especially those that our illness creates.

Yet having these thoughts does not make us abnormal or insane. Everyone has them to some degree. They are only thoughts and we do not have to act on them. If they do get too confusing or threatening, or if we begin to act on them, we can get help.

Do I manage the nagging thoughts that upset me today?

THOUGHT FOR THE DAY

Thoughts don't have to become actions.

WAITING FOR HEALING

We cannot rush the process of emotional or spiritual healing. Healing takes time and the guidance of our Higher Power.

Most of us want to be healed immediately and by the least painful method possible. But that is rarely how the process works.

Rather than demanding it be done at once, let us try a new approach. Let us remain patient and ask our Higher Power to heal us day by day.

Today, do I ask my Higher Power to help heal me one day at a time?

THOUGHT FOR THE DAY

Time, patience, and faith are the best healers.

IN THIS TOGETHER

We awake to our illness, just as we did yesterday and the day before that. We pour a cup of tea or coffee and realize that our illness will be our steady companion. We remind ourselves that we lived through yesterday—perhaps quite happily—and the day before that.

Yes, our illness will go through the day with us. But we have learned to manage it and live with it. We continue to recover one day at a time. And with the help of our Higher Power we are creating a new way of life for ourselves.

Today, do I deny my illness or do I accept it and work with it?

THOUGHT FOR THE DAY

I am strong and resilient and can manage my illness.

CHANGING TREATMENT

There are many treatments for mental illness, and researchers continue to discover new theories and medicines. Some treatments work well for certain people, yet are ineffective for others. A method that has worked well in the past may become ineffective in the future.

Our treatment may one day have to change. If so, we need to keep an open mind about new forms of treatment. We need to ask questions and listen carefully to what our doctor has to say. The more informed we are, the better off we are.

Do I keep an open mind about different types of treatment today?

THOUGHT FOR THE DAY

*Knowledge and flexibility can help me
take care of myself.*

GRATEFUL FOR WHAT WE HAVE

We may wonder whether what we have in our lives today is all there is to recovery, or all that we will ever have. We may wonder where the house or the money or the relationships have gone, or whether they will finally appear in our lives for the first time.

Sometimes this attitude comes more from self-pity than actual lack. What we may really need is gratitude for the gifts we have already been given.

If we search our souls, we will often discover that what we think we are missing in our lives is of lesser value than what we already have in our hearts. And when we put aside our wants and demands, we will discover that what we have within us and around us is what we've been looking for all along.

Do I focus on what I lack or am I grateful today for what I have?

THOUGHT FOR THE DAY

Each life has its own gifts and grace.

BEING THANKFUL

Although our life is far from perfect, we often feel hopeful and at peace, thanks to our own efforts, the help of others, and the grace of our Higher Power. With a recovery plan, opportunities have grown; fear of the present and future has faded.

Our life can take directions we could only dream of before we found recovery. Hope is more plentiful. Giving of ourselves has become more of a priority. Now, despite our illness, we are better able to live our life to its fullest.

Today, do I appreciate the good things in my life—without denying or sugar-coating the difficulties?

THOUGHT FOR THE DAY

Despite my illness, I can live a full and fruitful life.

WHO WE ARE RIGHT NOW

For many of us, there was a time when we were young and healthy. We felt more serene, capable, and secure. But when we were overcome by illness, all that changed. We felt alone, lost, and frightened of the future.

Today, our illness remains, but we are slowly recovering and coping as best we can. We may no longer be the person we once were, but we are grateful to our Higher Power for the gift of recovery and look forward to the future with courage, patience, and hope.

Today, do I love and accept the person I have become?

THOUGHT FOR THE DAY

Recovery means I focus on the present,
and love myself as I am right now.

SELF-ACCEPTANCE AND SELF-CONFIDENCE

Everybody feels inadequate at times. But when our illness took hold, most of us felt incapable of doing our normal tasks. We began to feel that we had let ourselves or others down.

Yet we need not judge ourselves by what we cannot do. Instead, let us look at what we can make of our gifts. As we learn more about our illness, we will accept ourselves more and develop more self-confidence.

Today, do I accept what I can and cannot do?

THOUGHT FOR THE DAY

As my recovery progresses, self-acceptance and self-confidence will grow.

PROGRESS, NOT PERFECTION

It helps to focus on progress rather than perfection. We can focus on creating better results rather than perfect results. We can accept ourselves and what we accomplish rather than shame ourselves for not being good enough (or as good as we once may have been).

Today, do I let go of perfection and focus on progress?

THOUGHT FOR THE DAY

With patience and effort, I can make progress.

MEDICATIONS AND RESPONSIBILITY

It is our responsibility to know just what medications are being offered to us. We need to know what effects and side effects they have, and how and why they work. We may need to ask our doctors about them or research them on our own.

Some of us cannot decide for ourselves because our illness is in complete control. But for those of us who are capable, it is our responsibility to ask questions and learn about our medications.

Am I taking responsibility for my medications today?

THOUGHT FOR THE DAY

*Taking responsibility for my medications
is an essential part of my recovery.*

Holiday Blues

Many of us can lose our emotional balance with the end-of-the-year holidays. We feel out of place. Some of us get depressed, some take to our rooms, and some of us get manic.

But the end of the year does not have to be filled with the blues. We can visit our friends and families. We can volunteer with organizations we believe in. We can join in religious or neighborhood activities. We can get support from others so that we are not alone and isolated.

Will I catch the holiday blues or can I connect with someone today?

Thought for the Day

I can celebrate the holidays in my own way and at my own pace.

LOOKING BEYOND OUR ILLNESS

Many of us could see nothing on the horizon but our illness and its symptoms. Yet learning to live with our illness requires that we look beyond our symptoms, that we face fears and doubts and learn to cope with them. Otherwise we cannot discover all that awaits us.

Looking beyond our illness takes courage and faith, but it can be done. Today let us begin to discover all that awaits us.

Can I begin looking beyond my illness today?

THOUGHT FOR THE DAY

Looking beyond my illness leads in a positive direction.

Overcoming Obstacles

The obstacles we face may seem overwhelming at times. But we need only look back at the obstacles we have already overcome—obstacles we once saw as insurmountable.

Then, as now, our Higher Power gives us the courage and strength we need. Whether smaller or larger, we will overcome each obstacle one by one.

Today, do I draw strength from the many obstacles I have already overcome?

Thought for the Day

An obstacle in my path does not destroy the path: I find a way over or around it, and my journey continues.

SUICIDE IS NO LONGER AN OPTION

Many of us with mental illness have used thoughts of suicide as a safety valve, a way to cope with our illness and our pain. Some of us have even tried suicide, perhaps multiple times. Yet we are still here.

Others are not so lucky. They reached a point where they felt they no longer had any options. But we do. One option is to promise ourselves—and at least one other person we care about—that suicide is no longer an option for us. We promise that we will seek alternatives the next time we think about taking our own life.

Today, do I remind myself that I always have options and that suicide is not one of them?

THOUGHT FOR THE DAY

Suicide is not an option.

ACCEPTING OUR LOSSES

Most of us with mental illness have lost friends and even family members. We also may have lost social or career abilities that were once second nature. Some of us have dealt with these losses and moved on. But some of us do not accept them, still stand in fear, and have yet to mourn.

If we don't mourn them, however, our feelings of loss can turn into anger, self-pity, shame, or resentment. If we do mourn them, we can move forward in our recovery and regain some of what we've lost.

Today, do I face and accept my losses?

THOUGHT FOR THE DAY

*There is no shame in shedding tears
for what I have lost.*

BEING VIGILANT

We can start down that slippery slope with hardly a clue. One day our defenses are down—we think all is well—and then down the slide we go. It can happen that fast, when we least expect it and with little or no warning.

To avoid that slope, we can't become complacent about managing our illness. It helps to get enough sleep, keep up with our daily medications, and stay in touch with our support people.

We must work to maintain all that we have gained. If we feel ourselves sliding, then we get help immediately.

Am I vigilant about my recovery today?

THOUGHT FOR THE DAY

The better I know myself,
the better I can take care of myself,
and the sooner I can get help when it's needed.

❄

Self-Sabotage

We all sabotage ourselves at times, often because deep down we feel undeserving because of our illness.

But having a mental illness doesn't make us any less of a person. It doesn't mean we don't deserve good things in life.

Mental illness is a brain disorder, not a failure of character; it's a no-fault illness just like diabetes or any other chronic physical condition.

Today, can I accept the good things that come my way and remind myself that I am worthy?

Thought for the Day

By accepting the good things in life,
I put my illness in its proper perspective.

WHEN PEOPLE FIND OUT

Many of us with a mental illness wonder what people will think and how will they react when they find out about our illness. Will they think we're crazy? Will they be confused or afraid? Will they accept us for who we are?

We need to remember that our self-worth does not depend on the acceptance of everyone we meet. More important is how we feel about ourselves, our illness, and our life. When we accept ourselves fully, then what others think about us will not worry us much.

Today, do I move ahead regardless of the fears and judgments of others?

THOUGHT FOR THE DAY

I cannot change how other people react to my illness;
I can change only how I see myself.

OUR SPECIAL DAY

We all need a special day once in a while; a day just for us. We take time for ourselves. We remind ourselves that we are lovable and loved, that we belong here on Earth, and that our Higher Power is always present to guide us. We take time to thank our Higher Power for who we are today.

Do I believe that I deserve the good things available to me today?

THOUGHT FOR THE DAY

I am important and I deserve the gift of a special day.

MAINTAINING PERSPECTIVE

All of us have good days and not-so-good days. When we are having a good day, we can write a letter to ourselves or make a journal entry, describing just how we're feeling. In it, we can explain why we feel good about ourselves, how we have accepted our illness, what our Higher Power means to us, and so on.

When we're feeling down, we can take out that writing and read it slowly. We can remind ourselves what it's like on our good days and what we have to look forward to.

If I'm feeling down today, do I remind myself of how I feel on my good days?

THOUGHT FOR THE DAY

Maintaining perspective can help ease my pain

GETTING ORGANIZED

When coping with a mental illness, we're bound to have days when we just can't get organized. We may forget things, lose things; we may have too many things to do and feel overwhelmed.

But it's not the end of the world. It's only one day.

Tomorrow we will have the chance to get up and try again. But this time, we can try to be more organized. We can write down what we have to do for that day and try not to do too much. With practice, more of our days can be organized.

Am I organized today? If not, can I be more organized tomorrow?

THOUGHT FOR THE DAY

Every day is a new start, a new opportunity.

HELPING OTHERS

Before we committed to a recovery plan, many of us were impatient and self-indulgent. We did whatever we wanted to do, to ourselves or others, at any time and any cost.

When the cost was more than we could pay, we got into recovery. We found spirituality (or it found us). We discovered that satisfying ourselves all the time made us unhappy, and that helping others brought us joy and peace.

What might I do today to make someone happy?

THOUGHT FOR THE DAY

Making others happy is spiritually rewarding.

GOOD CHANGE

Because of our mental illness, we have suffered some losses, such as freedom and flexibility. And because of our illness we suffer some new restrictions, such as avoiding alcohol and taking medication. The illness brings about both loss and change.

Loss is painful and most of us would avoid change if we could. But change may not be all bad. For example, as a result of our illness we can adopt a plan of recovery that allows us to get more sleep and more exercise. And we don't miss those extra calories in alcohol.

What is better in my life today because I have accepted my illness and begun to recover?

THOUGHT FOR THE DAY

After the upset change may cause,
there are often unforeseen benefits.

RETURNING HOME

Many of us who suffer from mental illness have yet to discover home—that place where we can learn to manage our illness and climb out of despair; where we are understood and loved. Such a place is possible for us all.

Those of us who have found this home are fortunate. We have what others are desperately searching for. Now, we show our gratitude by helping those who still struggle.

What can I do today to help others find their home?

THOUGHT FOR THE DAY

The search for home need not be a lonely journey.

DECEMBER

• DECEMBER 1 •

HOPE

Hope is a feeling, a belief, and a promise. It signals optimism and trust. Hope is what we rely on hour to hour and day to day.

Sometimes we lose hope. And sometimes hope appears when we least expect it, but need it the most. On the worst days, hope is what carries us to the better days ahead.

Is hope alive in my life today?

THOUGHT FOR THE DAY

Hope is a gift that I must never take for granted.

NOT JUDGING

Judging sets us apart. When we judge others, we are sure to be judged in return. When we hold others in contempt for their shortcomings or behavior, we can expect the same in return. This is especially a concern for anyone who lives with a mental illness.

But let us remember that we cannot judge others if we have not walked in their shoes. If we refrain from judging others, we will learn to more fully accept ourselves.

Today, do I focus on judging or acceptance?

THOUGHT FOR THE DAY

Before judging others, first look within.

• DECEMBER 3 •

SEEKING TRUTH

If we want to remain emotionally and spiritually healthy, we must continue to seek truth. We must be truthful with ourselves and others at all times. Granted, the truth can be painful. But it is truth that eventually sets us free.

For us, truth includes our illness and its limitations. But truth also includes our goals and dreams.

Am I completely honest today?

THOUGHT FOR THE DAY

The pain of truth gives way to the joy of freedom.

REGAINING THE TRUST OF FRIENDS AND FAMILY

We must acknowledge our past, that we know we were sick, if we want our loved ones to trust us again. If there were hospitalizations and suicide attempts, we know they were frightened and must have wondered many times if we would return. It's likely they watched from afar, helpless, as our illness took control of us.

But now we can ask that they have some faith in us. Faith that we have grown and learned to cope with our illness. Faith that we have learned from our past and that we are moving forward. But most important, know that we have developed faith in ourselves and in our Higher Power.

Have I found the faith that lies within me today— and have I shared this faith with others?

THOUGHT FOR THE DAY

Trust is earned from others.
Faith is a gift that comes from within.

• DECEMBER 5 •

CLAIMING A HIGHER POWER

It is hard to live with a mental illness—especially all alone. When we've been struggling on our own for some time, it's good to remind ourselves that we have help. We have a Higher Power.

Our Higher Power can be anything we want it to be. Whether it's the God of our religion or our recovery network, we need to experience a Power greater than ourselves to fully recover. We get to choose—as long as we believe there is something more powerful than we are that we can turn to for help and solace.

Our Higher Power is always there for us. We need only ask.

Today, do I touch base with my Higher Power?

THOUGHT FOR THE DAY

I don't have to go it alone anymore. I have help.

GETTING HELP IN THE MIDDLE OF THE NIGHT

For some of us with mental illness, the blackness of night can be the most frightening and lonely time. We wonder if anyone truly cares about us. We need to talk with someone; we need reassurance.

The good news is that many people can help us when we feel this way. We can call a crisis line. We can call a willing friend, someone in our support group, or a family member. We only need to pick up the phone and dial.

Will I reach out for help if I need it today, no matter what time it is?

THOUGHT FOR THE DAY

*Help is a phone call away if I do my part
in building my support network.*

Maintaining Hope

Many of us have fought successfully to regain our emotional, physical, and spiritual health. But for others of us the battle is not over and our days may be long and feel hopeless.

But let us not despair. Those who have regained balance in their lives teach us that recovery from mental illness is possible. We can recover as they did, one day at a time.

Let us seek the example of others and the support of our Higher Power to restore the faith and courage that lie within us.

Can I find a role model for hope today?

Thought for the Day

The things I look up to in other people are also within me.

• DECEMBER 8 •

HATING LIFE

There are times when we can hate our lives. We feel consumed by our illness and each day brings confusion. The hurt and shame can become unbearable and we wonder when it will stop.

But as the days go by, we may notice a slight shift. We can begin to accept the ways of our illness and its limitations. We begin to see that, though we can't necessarily do everything we could do before, we are doing a little more each day. We will eventually feel a little better and accept ourselves a little more each day.

Do I practice accepting my life and myself today?

THOUGHT FOR THE DAY

Despite what my illness may tell me,
I can love myself and my life again.

KNOWING OUR WARNING SIGNS

As we come to know ourselves and our illness, we become more aware of its warning signs. It is critical that we learn to see when we're on a downward spiral. For some of us it's a matter of life or death. If we know our warning signs, we can get the help we need before it is too late.

Do I know the warning signs of my illness and am I alert to them today?

THOUGHT FOR THE DAY

The better I know myself, the greater my chances for stability and healing.

ACKNOWLEDGING OUR ACHIEVEMENTS

Some of us are so focused on reaching the finish that we don't take the time to reward ourselves for what we have achieved today. Whether for doing a good job at work or being a good parent or making it through a tough day, we need—and deserve—to reward ourselves.

It doesn't have to be big—a peaceful walk, a relaxing bath, our favorite food or beverage. What is important is that we acknowledge our achievements and build some pleasure into our day.

Do I take time out to reward myself today?

THOUGHT FOR THE DAY

Reinforcing success builds self-esteem and confidence.

· DECEMBER 11 ·

FOLLOWING OUR DREAMS

Even though we have a mental illness, we still need dreams. Dreams help us get up each morning and can inspire us during the day.

It doesn't matter how far-fetched we think our dreams are; it doesn't matter how much we fear they will not come true. We can make progress on them day by day, despite ups and downs, obstacles (some caused by our mental illness), and getting off track from time to time. We just need to stay committed.

Am I following my dreams today?

THOUGHT FOR THE DAY

*Like recovery, realizing my dreams is a journey,
not a destination.*

MENTAL ILLNESS IS NOT A CHOICE

Mental illness is not a choice for any of us. It is a biochemical illness. And just like someone who has diabetes, or any other chronic condition, we must learn to live with our mental illness.

We can think of it as a constant burden or we can make peace with it. The choice is ours.

Today, do I realize that my illness was not a choice but that I can make peace with it?

THOUGHT FOR THE DAY

Having a mental illness is not a choice,
but living with it peacefully is.

• DECEMBER 13 •

JUST A PRAYER AWAY

When we are afraid and feel alone, it helps to remember that our Higher Power is but a prayer away. For those of us who aren't religious, prayer may mean asking for help from our support group or network. We are just a prayer away from acceptance and guidance, a prayer away from the courage and will to move forward on our journey.

Do I look to my Higher Power for strength and guidance today?

THOUGHT FOR THE DAY

When I seek guidance and direction
from my Higher Power, I am sure to find my way.

LIMITING OUR ANXIETY

We may often say to ourselves *I'm really nervous. Why can't I just relax?* Or, *I can't believe some of the things I do. What's wrong with me?* But these statements only put us down and produce more anxiety.

Yet if we can learn to live with our anxiety, it may begin to subside on its own.

It helps if we can talk to ourselves differently. Rather than giving ourselves negative messages, we can give ourselves positive ones such as *It's been worse before* or *This won't last forever* or *I will survive.* This self-talk can help us cope with our anxiety one day at a time.

Do I give myself helpful messages about my anxiety today?

THOUGHT FOR THE DAY

My anxiety may not completely leave me today, but I can learn to live with it.

• DECEMBER 15 •

HELPLESS

Anyone can become helpless temporarily, but if we remain helpless for any length of time, we may become one of the hopeless—someone who believes there are no answers and gives in to despair.

If we feel helpless, let us look for answers or solutions and then act on them before we become one of the hopeless. We need to learn how to become a survivor rather than a victim.

Today, do I make choices and take steps that support my recovery?

THOUGHT FOR THE DAY

Feeling helpless means it's time to look for help.

TRANSFORMING DESPAIR

Most of us are all too familiar with the despair our illness can bring about. For some of us, this feeling has come and gone. But for others, it has stayed—and it feels like forever.

Yet with practice, despair can change. When we reach out to other people and our Higher Power, we diminish the power of despair. As we practice reaching out, our mood will eventually lift.

Do I reach out today if I feel despair?

THOUGHT FOR THE DAY

Despair is an S.O.S. signal
for a Power greater than self.

BUYING MERCY

The pain and loneliness that mental illness brings about can be excruciating at times. For a little relief, many of us are tempted to try just about anything, including buying a little mercy—a pill, a bottle, a joint, or a needle.

We need to remember that mercy and salvation cannot be bought in any form. Mood-altering chemicals produce false relief and only put off our problems. If they briefly stop our immediate pain and loneliness, they only shift it to our future. They divert us from our journey of spirituality and recovery.

Where do I seek relief today?

THOUGHT FOR THE DAY

Mercy and salvation don't have a price.

SLOW BUT STEADY

Many of us with mental illness remember what it was like to be stuck in treatment for weeks at a time. We felt cooped up and frustrated. We wanted out. And no one could legally hold us!

But if we left, if we discharged ourselves without a doctor's approval, could we really manage on our own? Was the new medication at a therapeutic level? Had we learned our lessons from the last setback? Were we stable?

Then, as now, it makes sense to practice patience and trust the process.

Do I practice patience and trust today?

THOUGHT FOR THE DAY

Recovery is slow—slow but steady.

LONELINESS

Everyone gets lonely at times. That's the way life is. But those of us with mental illness may experience more than the average amount of loneliness. Soon we begin thinking that we will be lonely forever.

It helps to keep in mind that our loneliness will eventually pass. Rather than cling to it—like scratching a bug bite and making it worse—we can try to connect with other people and our Higher Power.

Do I see the choice I have today to connect with others and my Higher Power?

THOUGHT FOR THE DAY

Though loneliness is inevitable,
it need not be permanent.

RETURNING TO THE BASICS

As time passes, we may find ourselves slipping back into old habits. Perhaps our daily prayer and meditation become irregular or we no longer reach out to our support people or we stop attending support groups and working with others.

If we have fallen into such a pattern, today is the day to return to the basics that have guided and nurtured us thus far in our recovery.

If I have drifted away from the basics, can I return to them today?

THOUGHT FOR THE DAY

It is never too late to return to the basics of recovery.

CELEBRATING

The holidays are a time to celebrate. And alcohol is plentiful.

But rather than follow the crowd, let us keep in mind who we are and how much we can safely drink. Let us realize when to celebrate and when to take care of ourselves. Let us celebrate the holidays with those we love—and recognize our limitations.

Today, do I know how to take care of myself over the holidays emotionally, physically, and spiritually?

THOUGHT FOR THE DAY

Real joy can't be manufactured.

New Doors Open

As we continue on our journey, many doors will open for us. There will be doors of opportunity, of new freedom, and new relationships. Doors of acceptance and spiritual growth. Some doors will help us become humble, yet strong and self-confident. Some doors will hold growth and inner peace.

But the most important door is the one in front of us right now.

Today, do I open the door in front of me?

Thought for the Day

Each day is a phase on my journey,
a doorway to growth.

• DECEMBER 23 •

FEAR AND PRIDE

When we're feeling down or in turmoil or simply having a bad day, it's time to pick up the phone—and it's our responsibility to do so. Though our strength may be lacking, waiting for others to call does not help.

We may look at the phone and think *No one cares; otherwise they would call. Where are they? Don't they know I'm feeling bad?* But chances are they don't know that we are feeling bad. And staring at the phone won't make it ring.

For some of us, the hardest thing to do is ask for help in time of need. But we need to cast aside our fear and pride. We need to pick up the phone and dial.

Do I wait to be rescued today or do I reach out?

THOUGHT FOR THE DAY

In times of need, it is up to me to call for help.

RECOVERING TOGETHER

On our journey, we will learn that recovery is about *we*—not just *me*. In recovery we need each other for guidance and support. Together we can steadily grow stronger.

There are many of us with mental illnesses who are willing to share our recovery and give of ourselves. Let us walk together.

Today, do I remember that recovery is a "we" process rather than a "me" process?

THOUGHT FOR THE DAY

Recovering together creates
a powerful, long-lasting bond.

MIRACLES

We have risen above our darkness to embark on a new life, a new journey. In this life we can find peace. In this journey there is hope. *We are miracles of life.*

We have been given a gift from a source far greater than ourselves. Let us honor that source, and appreciate just how miraculous we are.

Do I realize that today, right now, I am a miracle?

THOUGHT FOR THE DAY

I am a survivor. I am recovering. I am a miracle

FREEDOM

Freedom is what most of us desire. We do not want to be prisoners of our illness. We want to wake up each morning knowing that the hours ahead are opportunities to live rather than events merely to survive.

How do we find and keep this freedom we desire? We can begin by accepting ourselves and our illness, and by connecting with our Higher Power. We can find freedom through the courage, faith, and wisdom our Higher Power gives us to use each day.

Today, have I turned to the source of freedom, my Higher Power?

THOUGHT FOR THE DAY

Freedom is granted to me when I recognize that my Higher Power is providing it every day.

MEDICATION IS NOT A CURE-ALL

Medications can be a key element in our recovery. Without them, the quality of life for many of us would be much lower.

But while medications can stabilize our moods, they cannot solve all our problems or make our life go as we would like it to. Rather, they can provide us with the balance and calmness we need to take responsibility for ourselves and our futures.

Do I rely strictly on medications for my recovery today or do I do my part as well?

THOUGHT FOR THE DAY

My recovery is spiritual, mental, and social as well as neurological.

KNOWLEDGE IS POWER

The more we know about our illness and its symptoms, the more choices we will have in our recovery, the better we will cope, and the healthier our decisions will be.

But knowledge does not fall out of the sky. We must look for it. We must be willing to learn and relearn.

Do I seek to learn about my illness today and put what I learn into action?

THOUGHT FOR THE DAY

*Knowledge is power, power that
can help heal and guide me.*

OUR TALENTS AND GIFTS

Whatever our talents and gifts, they deserve to be put to use. If we find ourselves with nothing to do and all day to do it, we could be putting our recovery, and our life, in danger.

Let us ask ourselves just what our talents are and how we can put them to use. Let's find out how we can enrich our lives and the lives of those around us.

Today, am I discovering or developing my talents and gifts?

THOUGHT FOR THE DAY

*I realize the true value of my talents
and gifts when I use them.*

PLANNING AHEAD

With a mental illness, we're bound to have days that aren't so good. That means we need to plan ahead. Thoughtful planning can save much grief—and may even save our lives.

We need to create a list of friends, family members, and professionals to call, including people who can visit us and help us get through these days. Planning ahead can save us from the worst effects of our illness.

While we're feeling our best, let us make plans for the future.

Can I do some planning today for those days when I'm feeling down?

THOUGHT FOR THE DAY

Prepare for the worst and expect the best.

• DECEMBER 31 •

THE PAST YEAR

This year was hardly perfect. (But neither were any of the ones before.) Still, it was a year of learning and relearning. It was a year of triumphs and setbacks; a year of spiritual growth and questions; a year in which we came to know ourselves and our illness better; a year that brought us greater self-acceptance; a year that offered us new freedom.

In this past year we also learned, yet again, that we must live in the present. And we learned, yet again, to be grateful.

Am I grateful today for all that has happened in my life this past year?

THOUGHT FOR THE DAY

My successes and setbacks of this past year give me strength and wisdom for the year ahead.

Index

Mark Allen Zabawa is a counselor and patient monitor for a large hospital. He suffers from bipolar disorder and has led dozens of support groups for those with mental health problems. He is the author of *Living with Chronic Pain One Day at a Time*.

Hazelden, a national nonprofit organization founded in 1949, helps people reclaim their lives from the disease of addiction. Built on decades of knowledge and experience, Hazelden offers a comprehensive approach to addiction that addresses the full range of patient, family, and professional needs, including treatment and continuing care for youth and adults, research, higher learning, public education and advocacy, and publishing.

A life of recovery is lived "one day at a time." Hazelden publications, both educational and inspirational, support and strengthen lifelong recovery. In 1954, Hazelden published *Twenty-Four Hours a Day,* the first daily meditation book for recovering alcoholics, and Hazelden continues to publish works to inspire and guide individuals in treatment and recovery, and their loved ones. Professionals who work to prevent and treat addiction also turn to Hazelden for evidence-based curricula, informational materials, and videos for use in schools, treatment programs, and correctional programs.

Through published works, Hazelden extends the reach of hope, encouragement, help, and support to individuals, families, and communities affected by addiction and related issues.

For questions about Hazelden publications, please call **800-328-9000**
or visit us online at **hazelden.org/bookstore**.